COLIN POWELL

"Have a Vision. Be Demanding."

Sandra H. Shichtman

Series Consultant:
Dr. Russell L. Adams, Chairman
Department of
Afro-American Studies,
Howard University

Enslow Publishers, Inc.

40 Industrial Road   PO Box 38
Box 398   Aldershot
Berkeley Heights, NJ 07922   Hants GU12 6BP
USA   UK

http://www.enslow.com

"HAVE A VISION. BE DEMANDING."
—Colin Powell

To my husband, Michael Shichtman,
for his encouragement and loving support

Library of Congress Cataloging-in-Publication Data

Shichtman, Sandra H.
    Colin Powell : "Have a vision. Be demanding" / Sandra H. Shichtman.
        p. cm. — (African-American biography library)
    Includes bibliographical references and index.
    ISBN 0-7660-2464-4 (hardcover)
    1. Powell, Colin L.—Juvenile literature. 2. Statesmen—United States—Biography—
Juvenile literature. 3. Generals—United States—Biography—Juvenile literature.
4. African American generals—Biography—Juvenile literature. 5. United States. Army—
Biography—Juvenile literature. I. Title. II. Series.
E840.8.P64S56 2005
973.931'092—dc22

                                                                          2004016799

Printed in the United States of America

10 9 8 7 6 5 4 3 2 1

To Our Readers:
We have done our best to make sure all Internet Addresses in this book were active and appro-
priate when we went to press. However, the author and the publisher have no control over and
assume no liability for the material available on those Internet sites or on other Web sites they
may link to. Any comments or suggestions can be sent by e-mail to comments@enslow.com or
to the address on the back cover.

Illustration Credits: AP/Wide World, pp. 3, 7, 25, 34, 39, 50, 57, 72, 74, 76, 78, 82, 84, 87, 89,
91, 93, 97, 100, 104, 106, 109, 113; City College of New York, p. 31; courtesy of Colin Powell,
pp. 13, 20, 29, 43, 46, 53, 60; Library of Congress, p. 4.

Cover Illustrations: AP/Wide World

Contents

Chapter 1

The Long Wait Ends

olin Powell was on an airplane headed to Washington, D.C., when a Supreme Court ruling that would affect his future was announced. "We got word as we landed that the Supreme Court had decided," he said. "I knew that night, as I landed at Dulles Airport, that I would be the next Secretary of State."[1] As secretary of state, Powell would serve as the principal foreign policy adviser to the president of the United States.

It was December 9, 2000. Five weeks earlier, the American people had voted for their forty-third president. The winner was not announced on Election Day. The Democratic candidate, Vice President Albert Gore, and the Republican candidate, George W. Bush, governor of Texas and son of a former U.S. president, were practically in a tie.

Florida's votes were needed to break the tie, but some

problems with the voting in Florida had made it impossible to announce a winner in that state. It appeared that George W. Bush had more votes than Albert Gore did, but the Democrats claimed that some of the votes meant for Gore had not been counted. They asked the Florida Supreme Court to order a recount of the votes. Then the Republicans appealed to an even higher court, asking the Supreme Court of the United States to stop the recount. Whoever was declared the winner in Florida would become the next president.

The nine justices of the Supreme Court handed down their ruling. There was to be no recount of the votes in Florida. As a result, George W. Bush won the election. He would be the next president of the United States.

Bush's decision to appoint Colin Powell as his secretary of state had been made during the long wait between the election and the announcement of the winner. "He and I had been talking during that period," Powell said. "He made it clear that, if he did defeat the Gore challenge, I would be the Secretary of State."[2]

A few days after Bush was declared the president-elect, Powell stood beside him at an elementary school near the Bush ranch in Crawford, Texas. Bush announced to the reporters gathered there, "Many times during the course of my campaign I said that if all went well General Colin Powell just might be called back into the service of his country. Today it is my privilege to make that call and ask him to become the sixty-fifth secretary of state of the United States of America."[3]

Powell thanked Bush and said that he was honored to have the opportunity to return to public service. He had been retired from public service for seven years. He told the president-elect, "I look forward to serving you, the American people, and the cause of peace and freedom around the world."[4]

Colin Powell made history in 2001 when he became the first African American to become secretary of state. At his right are President-elect George W. Bush and Vice President–elect Dick Cheney.

Powell still had to be approved by the United States Senate before he could be confirmed as the secretary of state. The Senate wanted to be sure that the secretary of state and the president-elect agreed on foreign policy. On January 17, 2001, he appeared before the Senate's Foreign Relations Committee. The senators asked Powell about his views on current issues such as what to do about Iraqi dictator Saddam Hussein, arms control talks with Russia, and a national missile defense system.[5]

Powell answered their questions. He also told them that as secretary of state he would support efforts to strengthen the North Atlantic Treaty Organization (NATO) and to establish new relationships with China, Russia, and North Korea.[6] The senators on the committee liked what Powell said. They were convinced that he would make a good secretary of state. They recommended that the full Senate confirm Powell.

Colin Powell became the secretary of state of the United States on January 22, 2001. He was the first African American to hold that position.

Chapter 2

A Childhood of Love, Learning, and Discipline

olin Luther Powell was born on April 5, 1937, in Harlem, a neighborhood in New York City. It was one of the few parts of the city that welcomed African Americans at that time. Harlem was home to thousands of African Americans, including immigrants from the Caribbean island of Jamaica. Colin, which his parents pronounced *Cah*-lin in the British manner, was the second child of Luther and Maud Ariel Powell. They also had a daughter, Marilyn, who was nearly six years old.

Both Luther and Maud had come from Jamaica. Like immigrants from other parts of the world, they moved to the United States seeking a better life for themselves and their children.

◆◆◆◆◆◆◆◆◆◆◆◆◆◆◆◆◆◆◆◆◆◆◆◆◆◆

Jamaica

Jamaica had been part of the British Empire since the 1600s. It became the biggest producer of sugar in the 1700s. In 1814 sugar production peaked at 34 million pounds.[1] Slaves were brought in from Africa to grow the sugarcane and to build homes and roads on the island. Jamaica had also become a major exporter of bananas by the middle of the 1800s. Twenty-one million stems of bananas were exported in 1927.[2] Jamaica's economy was thriving.

But political unrest on the island and natural disasters like hurricanes ruined Jamaica's economy. Tourism replaced sugar and bananas as the island's major industry. The island's wealth was concentrated in the hands of a few people. Everyone else worked at menial jobs or on small farms that produced only enough food for themselves. Wages were low and there were few good job opportunities. Many Jamaicans left the island to look for work in other countries.

Luther Theophilus Powell was one of nine children in a very poor farming family. His education was limited, and he never graduated from high school. His future in Jamaica looked hopeless. Luther left Jamaica in 1920, when he was in his early twenties. He arrived in the United States and worked as a gardener in Connecticut before moving to Harlem, New York. He found a job in the stockroom of Ginsburg's, a clothing manufacturer in New York City's garment center. Luther worked there for the next twenty-three years, rising from stock clerk to shipping department foreman.

Maud Ariel McKoy was also born in Jamaica. When she was a child, her mother left the island seeking a better life in New York City. After finding work as a maid and an apartment in Harlem, she sent for Maud, her eldest daughter. To help pay the bills, Alice and Maud rented out rooms in their apartment to boarders. The boarders paid rent weekly or monthly in exchange for a room and meals. One of the boarders in the McKoys' apartment was Luther Powell.

Luther and Maud fell in love. After they married, they moved into their own apartment on Morningside Avenue in Harlem. Their children, Marilyn and Colin, were born there. The family remained in Harlem until Colin was four years old.

By then the neighborhood had changed. The local public schools were not very good. The West Indian immigrant families who lived in Harlem knew that the key to a better life for their children was a good education. So they began looking at other areas of New York City, where the public schools were better. Many Jamaican families moved out of Harlem. They settled in a part of the city called the Bronx. The public schools in the Bronx would give their children a better education. The Powells followed their neighbors from Harlem to the Bronx and settled in the South Bronx.

In 1943, when Colin was six years old, the Powells moved into an apartment on the third floor of a four-story apartment building on Kelly Street. It was in a section of the South Bronx called Hunts Point. Some of Luther and Maud's relatives were already living there. Both Luther and Maud worked in the garment center, and their children were looked after by aunts, uncles, and cousins.

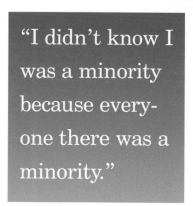

"I didn't know I was a minority because everyone there was a minority."

Hunts Point was very different from Harlem. Hunts Point was home to a variety of people, mostly European Jews but also Italians, Puerto Ricans, Poles, and African Americans. It was a neighborhood of small *bodegas* (grocery stores), butcher shops, Italian restaurants, Jewish delicatessens, and Chinese laundries. Colin later said, "I didn't know I was a minority because everyone there was a minority."[3]

Hunts Point had its share of problems as well. Empty buildings had been torn down, leaving lots that quickly filled with garbage, broken glass, and rats. Drugs were sold on street corners and there were often fights between rival street gangs.

Colin never got into any trouble. "When I set off to school each morning, I had an aunt in every other house,

Colin, age seven or eight.

"I lacked drive, not ability. I was a happy-go-lucky kid."

stationed at the window with eyes peeled, ready to spot the slightest misbehavior on my part and report it back to my parents," he wrote many years later.[4] He stayed away from drugs because he knew his parents would punish him severely if he did not.[5]

Colin learned early on how to get along with boys and girls from different backgrounds. He had friends who were Puerto Rican, African American, and Jewish. They rode bicycles, flew kites from their rooftops in summer, and played stickball, punchball, and stoopball outdoors when weather permitted. This ability to get along with others would be a valuable skill for Colin in his later life.

As a young boy, Colin was not a very good student. When he entered fourth grade at Public School 39, he was put into a class for slow learners. He later said, "I lacked drive, not ability. I was a happy-go-lucky kid."[6] But even from an early age, he knew that his parents expected him to go to college. They believed that the only way for their children to get ahead in the world was to get a college education.

After the United States entered World War II in December 1941, many young men from Hunts Point volunteered or were drafted into the army to fight for their country. Like the other boys in the neighborhood, Colin was fascinated by the stories he heard about America's fighting forces. "I deployed legions of lead soldiers and

Pearl Harbor Brings U.S. Into World War II

When World War II began in Europe in 1939, the United States declared itself a neutral country, not taking sides. But in 1941, Japan pulled the United States into the war. Conflict between Japan and the U.S. had been brewing for a number of years.

In the 1930s, Japan had invaded China, Korea, and other nations in Southeast Asia. The United States demanded that Japan withdraw. When it did not, the U.S. stopped doing business with Japan. In 1941, the Japanese government feared that the powerful U.S. Navy would force Japan to leave the nations it had conquered. So Japan decided to destroy the U.S. Pacific Fleet.

The U.S. Naval Base was located in Pearl Harbor, Hawaii. In the early hours of December 7, 1941, Japanese ships and airplanes bombed Pearl Harbor in a surprise attack. Almost twenty-five hundred sailors were killed and nearly two thousand were wounded.

The American people were angry. They demanded that the United States do something about the attack. "Remember Pearl Harbor," Americans said as their nation entered World War II. The United States joined Great Britain, China, the Soviet Union, and more than forty other countries in fighting and defeating Japan, Italy, Germany, and six smaller nations.

directed battles on the living-room rug," he later wrote.[7]

It was during that time that Colin's friends changed the way they said his first name. A fighter pilot named Colin P. Kelly Jr. became an American hero when his plane was shot down while on a bombing raid on a Japanese warship. Captain Kelly's first name was pronounced *Coh*-lin. So Colin's friends started calling him *Coh*-lin. His parents and family continued to call him *Cah*-lin.[8]

The World War II years were good for Luther and Maud Powell. With so many people off fighting the war, jobs were plentiful for those who remained at home. Luther Powell rose early each morning, dressed in a suit and tie, perched a hat on his head, and rode the subway to his job in downtown New York City. He did not arrive back home until seven or eight o'clock in the evening.

Maud Powell worked as a seamstress for a garment center company. Like many other women who wanted to earn extra money, she also did piecework sewing at home. She sewed buttons and trimmings on clothing and was paid for each completed piece. Every Friday, she removed the tags from the completed pieces, bundled them together, and rode downtown on the subway to the garment center. She handed the tags to her boss and was paid for her work.

With both parents working, the Powells could afford to give their children music lessons. Colin took piano lessons for a while and then switched to the flute. When it was agreed that he had no talent for playing either instrument, the lessons were discontinued.

Gene Norman was one of Colin's closest friends. He lived across the street from the Powells on Kelly Street. Although he was two years older than Colin, the boys had a lot in common. "We both came from West Indian families," Gene Norman said. "We both seemed interested, like so many other kids, in the war that was going on and we made ourselves knowledgeable about that. And Colin was a very loyal friend, somebody that you could trust."[9]

Colin liked playing sports, but he was not a good athlete. "Stickball was an important game in the Bronx in those days," said Norman. "Colin wasn't a very good stickball player. He wasn't a great hitter and he wasn't a great fielder either. But he could run pretty fast."[10] Colin would not find out what he was really good at doing until he entered college many years later.

At Junior High School 72, Colin was a popular student. His leadership qualities began to emerge. He was elected captain of his class. But his grades were just average. He graduated from the ninth grade in June 1950, just days before North Korean troops invaded South Korea. America was drawn into another war. Colin and his friends had been interested in all the details of World War II. Now they became fascinated by the Korean War.

Colin became a student at Morris High School in September 1950. The school was just a few blocks from

The Korean War

When Japan was defeated in World War II, the U.S. and the Soviet Union divided Korea at the 38th parallel, an imaginary line that cuts through Korea. The top part, North Korea, became a communist country, and the lower part, South Korea, a democracy.

On June 25, 1950, North Korean soldiers invaded South Korea. The United Nations (U.N.) demanded that the North Koreans return to their own country. When they refused, U.N. member-nations, including the United States, sent soldiers and supplies to help South Korea defeat the invaders. China and the Soviet Union sent soldiers to help the North Koreans.

During the three years of the war, more than 2 million soldiers died. On July 27, 1953, North Korea signed a United Nations agreement, promising to stop fighting. A peace treaty between North Korea and South Korea was never signed. U.S. troops remained in South Korea even after the war, and soldiers still guard the border today.

his house, and he could walk back and forth each day. His grades did not improve during the three and a half years he spent in high school. He was still just an average student.

Colin got a part-time job when he was fourteen years

old. His friend Gene already worked after school and on Saturdays at Siegel's, a small neighborhood store. Siegel's sold baby carriages and cribs. Colin wanted to know if there was room for two part-time workers at Siegel's. There was not, but Mr. Siegel, the store owner, suggested that Colin try up the block at Sickser's.[11]

Sickser's was a larger store that also sold cribs and baby carriages as well as high chairs and toys. Colin was hired to unload furniture and toys, display them in the store, and box them up again after they were sold. Sickser's customers were mainly Jewish people who spoke Yiddish. So Colin learned to speak a little Yiddish while working in the store.

What Colin enjoyed most during his high school years was hanging out with his friends. One of their favorite pastimes was walking to the local business area, with its wide variety of stores. The shop windows displayed interesting and exciting things to buy if you had the money.

Colin and his friends would go to the Tiffany movie theater every Saturday morning. There they watched a serial, which was an adventure movie shown one segment a week. Two cowboy movies followed each segment.

Gene Norman later said: "One way we used to get enough money for the admission as well as popcorn and candy was to collect returnable soda and beer bottles. We would go around to people that we knew, collect their

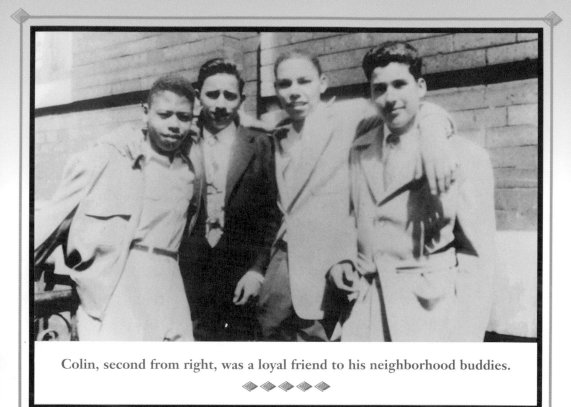

Colin, second from right, was a loyal friend to his neighborhood buddies.

bottles, turn them in, and end up with a pocketful of change to go off to the movie."[12]

Colin graduated from high school in January 1954. He knew that college was the next step for him, just as it had been for his sister, Marilyn. "I went to college for a single reason: my parents expected it," he said.[13]

Marilyn had attended Buffalo State Teacher's College in upstate New York. She majored in bilingual education and graduated in 1952. Now it was Colin's time to go to college. He applied to New York University and City College of New York, and both schools accepted him.

Chapter 3

A College Student's Commitment

T he decision about which college to enter was an easy one. The Powells could not afford to send Colin to New York University. They did not have $750 a year for college tuition there. But they *could* afford to send him to City College, which cost only $10 a year. So Colin Powell enrolled at City College.

He set off by bus one February morning in 1954 for his first day at college. He was sixteen and a half years old. "I was overwhelmed," Colin later said. "And then I heard a friendly voice: 'Hey, kid, you new?'"[1]

The voice belonged to Raymond the Bagel Man, who sold pretzels from a cart near the school. Colin bought a pretzel and chatted with Raymond for a few minutes. He had made his first friend even before reaching the gray stone buildings of City College.

Colin started his college career as an engineering major. It was not that he loved the idea of becoming an engineer, someone who plans, designs, and builds bridges, roads, and buildings. He really had no idea about his future career. But his mother thought that engineering would be an excellent choice for him. "That's where the money is," she told him.[2] She wanted him to be able to get a good job when he graduated.

Colin managed to get a B average in his first semester at City College. He was still working at Sickser's on weekends and during school vacations. But he decided that he was not earning enough money there to pay for his books and other necessities.

So Colin got a job that summer at a Pepsi Cola bottling plant in Long Island City. He also took a mechanical drawing course at City College. Mechanical drawing—that is, drawing with tools such as a compass, protractor, or T-square—was one of the required courses for engineering students.

When the mechanical drawing teacher asked the students to draw "a cone intersecting a plane in space," Colin had no idea what to do. He decided then that he was not meant to become an engineer.[3]

Colin's job at the Pepsi plant was a disappointment as well. He had been hired as a porter, given the task of mopping the floors. He was taught the proper way to mop—left to right, not back and forth. Colin noticed that all the porters in the plant were African American and that all the workers on the bottling machines were white. This offended him, but he decided to say nothing. "As Black teenagers, we were very much aware of segregation and what that meant, even though it wasn't practiced anywhere as overtly in New York as it was down South," said Colin's friend Gene Norman years later. "But certainly we'd heard about it and it was a matter of discussion at family dinners and family get-togethers."[4]

Segregation

Segregation keeps groups of people apart from each other because of their race, their religion, or the culture they come from. For a long time, racial segregation existed by law in many places in the United States, especially in the South. African Americans could not eat in the same restaurants, go to the same schools, or drink from the same water fountains as white people. On buses, they had to sit in the back and give up their seat if a white person was standing.

Colin decided to be the best porter he could possibly be. His hard work did not go unnoticed. At summer's end, the foreman told him, "Kid, you mop pretty good." Colin replied, "You gave me plenty of opportunity to learn."[5] The foreman invited Colin to return again the following summer. Colin said he would like to come back, but only if he could work on the bottling machines. The foreman promised him that he could.

Colin switched his major to geology when college resumed in fall 1954. Geology, the study of rock formations, interested him more than engineering had. But he still did not know what his future career would be.

Reserve Officer Training Corps

ROTC was first established at City College in 1916, when World War I was about to begin. It started as a training course to prepare students to join the army after graduation. Besides classroom instruction, ROTC members, called cadets, spent one summer at an army training camp. ROTC units appeared in many other colleges across the country.

By the 1950s, ROTC had become very popular on college campuses. The unit at City College was the second largest one in the country (not counting the units at military colleges).

One day, Colin noticed a group of students marching in step, one behind the other, on the campus. They wore military uniforms of olive-drab pants and jackets, brown shirts and ties, and brown shoes. They were members of the Reserve Officer Training Corps (ROTC).

In fall 1954, Colin Powell joined the ROTC at City College. "I am not sure why," he said later. "Maybe it was growing up in World War II and coming of age during the Korean conflict."[6] As a boy, he had seen war movies and listened to his parents and relatives talk about those wars.

There was yet another reason. None of his friends from Kelly Street were enrolled in college. His friend Gene Norman had enlisted in the Marine Corps. Colin and Norman could see each other only when Norman came home on leave or for weekends. Then they would go to a restaurant about a block away from home and order pizza and a beer.[7] At the time, pizza was a novelty food, and not many restaurants in their neighborhood served it.

When Colin first saw ROTC cadets like these,
he knew immediately that he wanted to join their ranks.

Colin's other Kelly Street friends thought it a little weird to see him wearing an ROTC uniform. "But they took it in stride," he said. "They didn't harass me, and I cut a pretty smart figure in my uniform. I didn't look like a dork."[8] Some of his friends even gave him a nickname, Soldier Boy.[9]

Colin had felt isolated and alone at City College. Wearing the ROTC uniform gave him a sense of belonging. He liked the sense of order that being in the military gave him. He also joined a group within ROTC called the Pershing Rifles.

The Pershing Rifles was a precision drill team and honor guard. Its cadets carried rifles, moving them from shoulder to shoulder in precise repetitions as they marched. Pershing Rifles cadets also marched in parades, carrying flags. Many Pershing Rifles cadets planned a career in the army after graduation. "That appealed to me," Colin wrote later.[10]

He had finally found a place where he felt comfortable. In ROTC, his talents could shine—and he was among people who could appreciate those talents. "If this is what soldiering was all about, then maybe I wanted to be a soldier," he wrote later.[11]

Colin liked the discipline and structure of the Pershing Rifles. He found friends among its members and became a leader almost immediately. Although he still was barely passing his other college courses, he began getting straight A's in his ROTC courses.

One of the Pershing Rifles cadets was Ronald Brooks, another African-American student. Ronald was two years ahead of Colin and became his adviser, role model, and friend. As Ronald moved up into higher positions within the Pershing Rifles, Colin took over the positions he left. Colin learned a valuable lesson from Ronald: Lead by example.[12] It was a principle that he would follow throughout his college and army careers.

> Colin finally found a place where he felt comfortable— and where his talents could shine.

Colin returned to the Pepsi Cola bottling plant in Long Island City for the summer of 1955. As the foreman had promised, Colin was set to work on the bottling machines. He so impressed his employers that he became deputy shift leader by the end of the summer.

The South Bronx was changing. Older residents who had saved up some money moved out. Poorer people moved into the empty apartments. Many landlords could no longer afford to make repairs and improvements to their buildings. They began to abandon some of those buildings. Drugs and guns appeared in the neighborhood.

Luther and Maud Powell decided that it was time to move their family out of the South Bronx. Many of their neighbors and family members had moved to better neighborhoods in the Upper Bronx or in the borough of Queens. In 1956 the Powells bought a three-bedroom house on Elmira Avenue in Hollis, Queens. Luther Powell was proud to own his own home, but Maud worried about how they would pay back the money the bank had lent them to buy the house.

During his junior year, Colin enrolled in advanced ROTC courses. He became a pledge officer. Pledges were students who wanted to join the Pershing Rifles. They had always been recruited with pornographic movies and offers of beer. Colin changed this. Instead, as pledge officer, he showed movies about what the Pershing Rifles did. It was such a success that the Pershing Rifles signed up more new cadets than ever before—twenty-one students joined.[13]

When the City College ROTC unit took part in a regional competition with units from other colleges in the spring of 1957, Ronald Brooks was in charge of the Pershing Rifles' regular drill team. Colin led the trick drill team. Both teams spent every spare moment preparing for the event, and both teams came in first in the competitions.

That summer Colin spent six weeks in Fort Bragg, North Carolina, for military training. He worked hard firing rifles and mortars and learning the art of camouflage. At the end of six weeks, honors were awarded to the cadets who had performed best. Colin was honored as Best

At ROTC summer camp in 1957,
Colin was named Best Cadet, Company D.

Cadet, Company D, which meant that he was the second-best cadet at camp. A white cadet had won the top honor. A sergeant explained to Colin that an African-American cadet could never be named Best Cadet in camp because of the color of his skin. "You think these Southern ROTC instructors are going to go back to their colleges and say that the best kid here was a Negro?" the sergeant asked Colin.[14]

This was Colin's first real experience with racism—disliking a person because of the color of his or her skin. But it would not be his last. Colin drove back to New York with two white cadets. On the way, they stopped at gas stations with segregated rest rooms. The bathrooms were clearly marked MEN, WOMEN, and COLORED. Colin had to use the COLORED rest rooms. This was very upsetting to Colin, who had grown up in an integrated neighborhood in the North. "I did not start to relax until we reached Washington, didn't feel safe until we were north of Baltimore," he said later.[15]

Back at college, Colin continued getting mediocre grades in his academic courses, but straight A's in ROTC. Ronald Brooks had graduated from City College, and Colin was now in charge of both the regular drill team and the trick drill team. He became a cadet colonel and led the entire City College ROTC.

Colin learned another valuable lesson when his ROTC unit again competed against units from other colleges. He was aware that his trick team leader was not fully prepared to enter the competition. Still, the leader assured Colin that he could do the job, and Colin did not remove him. When the City College trick drill team lost, Colin regretted his decision. "I learned that being in charge means making decisions, no matter how unpleasant."[16]

> "I learned that being in charge means making decisions, no matter how unpleasant."

Colin Powell graduated from City College with a degree in geology and a commission as second lieutenant in the army.

On June 9, 1958, Colin received his commission as a second lieutenant in the United States Army. His straight-A grades in ROTC earned him the honor of being chosen a Distinguished Military Graduate. He would have to serve in the army for the next three years. He received his college degree in geology at graduation the next day.

Colin's parents expected him to put in his three years in the army, then come home and begin his career. Little did they know that their son's career had already begun.

Chapter 4

"You're in the Army Now"

Powell was sent to Fort Benning, Georgia, for five months of army training. It was June 1958. Powell was twenty-one years old and making his second trip to the South.

First he took basic infantry training, reviewing some skills he had learned at ROTC and in the Pershing Rifles. They included firing and cleaning a rifle, finding and fighting the enemy, and avoiding being captured by the enemy. Powell was one of the top ten students in his class.

Next came Ranger training. Powell's unit went on long marches and spent nights in the swamps carrying heavy backpacks and machine guns or rifles as part of this especially difficult training. One evening when his unit was out on a march, Powell and another trainee, William McCaffrey, were assigned to carry the machine guns. Another Ranger trainee took the heavy machine gun from

**Like these soldiers, Powell had to learn parachute jumping—
though it was a skill that he did not enjoy.**

Powell after a while and gave him a rifle to carry instead.
The rifle did not weigh as much as the machine gun
did. Powell soon exchanged the rifle for the machine
gun McCaffrey was carrying. "I'll never forget that,"
McCaffrey said later.[1]

After Ranger training, Powell signed up for Airborne
training, which included learning to jump out of an airplane with a parachute. "If I never have to parachute
again, that will be fine with me, yet there was never any

doubt in my mind that I would do what had to be done," he wrote years later.[2]

During his time at Fort Benning, Powell came to understand the reality of racial segregation. His being African American was not an issue as long as he remained on the base. It was entirely different when Powell went into the nearby city of Columbus, Georgia. There, as in other places in the South, African Americans were still treated like second-class citizens. "I could go into Woolworth's in Columbus, Georgia, and buy anything I wanted, as long as I did not try to eat there," Powell later wrote. "I could go into a department store and they would take my money, as long as I did not try to use the men's room."[3]

This was a far cry from the way Powell had been brought up. His neighbors in the Bronx had come from many different countries of the world. It did not matter if their skin was white or brown or black. Everyone was treated equally in his neighborhood.

Powell was determined not to let racism in the South affect him or his feelings about himself. He had come to Fort Benning to do a job, and he would do that job to the best of his ability.

> "If I never have to parachute again, that will be fine with me, yet there was never any doubt in my mind that I would do what had to be done."

Racial Segregation Ends on Military Bases

Executive Order 9981, signed by President Harry S. Truman on July 26, 1948, made racial segregation illegal in the U.S. Armed Forces. Military personnel could no longer be separated according to their race on any military base in the United States.

Before that, African-American soldiers and officers did not serve in the same units as white soldiers and officers. They slept in separate bunks and ate in separate dining rooms. They did not use the same bathrooms or showers. By the time Powell arrived in Fort Benning, the military was fully integrated.

When Powell completed his training at Fort Benning, he received his orders to go to West Germany. He was stationed at an army post less than fifty miles from East Germany. It was his first field command, and, as a second lieutenant, he was put in charge of forty soldiers.

West Germany was a dangerous place to be at that time. It was the height of the Cold War. Soldiers from the Soviet Union might attack West Germany at any moment by coming over the border from East Germany.

While he was in West Germany, Powell was ordered to prosecute three army truck drivers. Their reckless driving had caused the deaths of three German civilians. Powell had never studied law, but now he had to learn military law to do his job. He got convictions for two out of the three truck drivers.

That experience taught Powell something important about himself. He learned that he had the ability to read a lot of information, process it, and talk intelligently to others about it. He could also persuade others to agree with his point of view.

Powell was promoted to first lieutenant in late December 1959. In the summer of 1960, he got his first taste of the destruction a war causes. An artillery shell accidentally hit a tent on the army base and exploded. Twelve soldiers were killed and more were injured. Body parts were everywhere. This was nothing like the war movies Powell had seen as a child.

> "I could go into Woolworth's in Columbus, Georgia, and buy anything I wanted, as long as I did not try to eat there. I could go into a department store and they would take my money, as long as I did not try to use the men's room."

Powell voted for the first time in the presidential election of November 1960. Democrat John Fitzgerald Kennedy ran against Republican Richard M. Nixon. The Democrats tended to appeal to minority voters, and Powell's vote went to Kennedy.

Powell's two-year stint in West Germany ended about

Communism and the Cold War

Communism is a form of government where farms, factories, newspapers, TV and radio stations, and all other kinds of property are owned by the government, rather than by individual people.

Communism came to the Soviet Union after a revolution in Russia in 1917. By the end of World War II, the Soviet Union occupied many countries in Eastern Europe. Millions of people lived under Communist rule.

The Soviet Union and the United States, known as the superpowers, were suspicious of each other. The Soviet Union accused the United States of wanting to build an empire. The United States warned the Soviet Union against spreading Communism around the world. Each country began to build and stockpile weapons, including nuclear missiles, in case the other attacked.

The tension between the two countries was known as the Cold War because it was not a war of fighting, but a power struggle of spying, mistrust, and opposing political ideas.

that time as well. The army ordered him back to the United States. Powell had liked being based in West Germany. He called it "a breath of freedom" for African Americans, especially those from the South. "They could go where they wanted, eat where they wanted, and date whom they wanted, just like other people," he said.[4]

The army sent him to Fort Devens, Massachusetts, about thirty miles outside Boston. First Lieutenant Colin Powell arrived there in January 1961. By summer of that year, Powell had completed his three years of army service. His obligation was over, and he could have left the army. But Powell never considered doing that. He loved the army and decided to make it his career. He also

During the Cold War, United States soldiers helped patrol the borders, like this one between East and West Germany.

◆◆◆◆◆

thought "the only place a black man could go all the way to the top was the military."[5] He told his parents that he was not coming home.

It was while he was at Fort Devens that Powell met Alma Johnson. They were on a double date arranged by his friend Mike Heningburg in November 1961. Heningburg had asked his girlfriend to bring along a friend to be Powell's date.

Alma Johnson was a graduate student at Emerson College in Boston. She was studying audiology, the science of hearing. She also worked at the Boston Guild for the Hard of Hearing as an audiologist, testing people's hearing. Alma was not anxious to go out with Powell when she heard he was a soldier. But she finally agreed.

> "The only place a black man could go all the way to the top was the military."

Alma had been born in 1937 in Birmingham, Alabama, and was raised there. Her father, Robert Johnson, was the principal of Parker High School, one of only two high schools for African Americans in Birmingham. Her mother, Mildred Johnson, had founded the Girl Scouts for African-American girls in Birmingham. Alma had attended the segregated schools of Birmingham and then Fisk University in Nashville, Tennessee. She had graduated from Fisk at the age of nineteen and moved north to Boston.

Powell liked Alma Johnson from their very first date.

Alma later said, "We had a wonderful time, and I thought he was the nicest man I ever met, but not really my type."[6] Still, she began going out with him on a regular basis. Powell would drive to Boston from Fort Devens to see her and then drive back to the base afterward.

By the summer of 1962, Powell had been at Fort Devens for eighteen months. In June he was promoted to captain. He received his orders in August; he was being sent to Vietnam for a year.

Powell called his parents and friends with the news that he was going to Southeast Asia. When he called Alma, she was not happy about it. She told Powell that unless they got married first, she would not write to him or wait for him to return from Vietnam. Powell was in love with Alma, so he asked her to marry him.

The wedding was to take place in Birmingham in August 1962. Luther Powell, Colin's father, said he would not come to the wedding. He wanted no part of the racist, segregated city of Birmingham.

Colin's mother, Maud Powell, did plan to attend. Colin's sister, Marilyn, and her husband, Norman, who was white, also said they would be there, traveling south from their home in Buffalo, New York. When Luther heard that his daughter and son-in-law were going to Birmingham, he changed his mind and decided to go after all. He was concerned that Marilyn and Norman, as an interracial couple, might need his protection. Interracial

◆◆◆◆◆◆◆◆◆◆◆◆◆◆◆◆◆◆◆◆◆◆◆◆◆◆◆◆

Vietnam

Vietnam is a country in Southeast Asia. It had been part of Indochina, a colony that belonged to France. But rebel forces in Indochina fought for and won their independence from France in 1954. Indochina was then divided into three countries—Vietnam, Laos, and Cambodia. Vietnam was divided into two parts. The top half, North Vietnam, was controlled by people who favored Communism. The bottom half, South Vietnam, had a more democratic form of government.

Some rebel forces in South Vietnam wanted a Communist government there. They were called Vietcong. The United States began sending military advisers to South Vietnam to help build up its army. They hoped that a strong South Vietnamese army would keep the Vietcong and their allies from overthrowing the democratic government.

marriages were illegal in the South at that time, and he worried about how they would be treated.

Colin Powell and Alma Johnson were married on August 25, 1962. They reported to Fort Bragg, North Carolina, about a month later. There, Colin began the Military Assistance Training Adviser course, which had to be completed before he could be sent to Vietnam.

Colin Powell and Alma Johnson had a big wedding in Birmingham.

Because it was only a six-week course, the army could not provide family housing for him and Alma at Fort Bragg. So the newlyweds looked for a place to live in Fayetteville, North Carolina, just outside Fort Bragg. Like other towns and cities in the South, Fayetteville was still segregated by race. The housing in the section of town where African Americans lived was shabby and run-down.

When they could not find proper housing of their own, the Powells moved in with some white friends, Joe and Pat Schwar and their children. Colin had served in West Germany with Joe Schwar. By then, Colin and Alma Powell were expecting their first child.

Chapter 5

Two Tours of Duty in Vietnam

The Powells stayed with the Schwars for the six weeks of the Military Assistance Training Adviser course. At Fort Bragg, Powell studied the history of Vietnam and why the United States was sending advisers to that country. He also learned some words in the Vietnamese language. Then he took Alma home to Birmingham. She would live there with her parents while Colin was in Vietnam.

Powell arrived in South Vietnam in December 1962. He was sent to the A Shau Valley, near the border of Laos. His job as an adviser was to teach soldiering skills such as rifle shooting and patrol tactics to a unit of the South Vietnamese army and to help with disciplinary problems among its members.

Powell accompanied his unit into the dense, steamy jungle as they searched for Vietcong. Their job was to

Captain Colin Powell, left, with two of his soldiers in Vietnam.

❖ ❖ ❖ ❖ ❖

keep the Vietcong from bringing weapons, ammunition, and supplies from North Vietnam into South Vietnam and Laos. Being out in a real combat situation was exciting to Powell until he began seeing dead and wounded soldiers. As he had discovered in West Germany: "This is not war movies on a Saturday afternoon; it was real, and it was ugly," he said.[1]

The Powells' baby was due to be born while Colin was away in Vietnam. So Colin and Alma devised a plan to let

Colin know that he had become a father. The plan was that Alma would write the words "Baby Letter" on the envelope of her letter when the baby was born. Colin advised the mail handler in Vietnam to be on the lookout for an envelope addressed to him with those words on it. When the letter came, the mail handler was supposed to immediately send a radio message to Colin to give him the news.

Alma sent the "Baby Letter," but it was never opened, and the radio message never came. The letter was mixed in with unsorted letters for hundreds of other American soldiers in Vietnam. Only a postscript at the bottom of a letter from Powell's mother told him that he was a father. "Oh, by the way, we are absolutely delighted about the baby," Maud Powell wrote.[2] Michael Kevin Powell had been born in Birmingham on March 23, 1963.

Six months after Colin Powell arrived in Vietnam, he and his unit were on patrol and walking in a creek. Powell stepped on a punji stick trap the Vietcong had stuck into the creek bed. The stick had a sharp point that had been dipped in poisonous animal dung. The punji stick went through Powell's boot and into his right foot. His foot swelled up and turned purple.

He received medical treatment for his wound. He also received a Purple Heart, the medal the army gives to soldiers who are wounded in the line of duty.

The army did not send Powell back to his unit in the A Shau Valley when he recovered from his wound. His year of service was almost over and it would soon be time for him to go home. So the army assigned him to its headquarters in Hue. "It would be dishonest to say I hated to leave combat," Powell wrote.[3]

The army sent Powell back to the United States in November 1963. On November 22, he was at an airport in Nashville, Tennessee, waiting for his flight to Birmingham. He learned from TV reports that President Kennedy had been shot and killed in Dallas, Texas.

Powell went home to Alma and his son. Michael was already eight months old. Birmingham was far different from the city he had left. "I had returned home, it seemed, to a world turned upside down," he said later.[4] The schools of Birmingham had been integrated during the year he was in Vietnam. But in September, not long before his return, a bomb had exploded in an African-American church in Birmingham, killing four little girls.

"I had returned home, it seemed, to a world turned upside down."

Powell was assigned again to Fort Benning, where he was scheduled to take the Infantry Officers Advanced Course in August 1964, nearly eight months away. He needed to find a place for himself and his family to live until then. Once the course began, the Powells could live on-base at Fort Benning. In the

The Civil Rights Movement

The African-American struggle for civil rights gathered momentum in the 1960s. The Supreme Court had ruled against segregation in public schooling and on city buses, but many whites in the South refused to comply with the laws. In 1960, civil rights activists in Greensboro, North Carolina, staged the first "sit-in," taking seats at a whites-only lunch counter and refusing to move. They were peaceful, polite, and determined. Sit-ins spread across the South. In 1961, "Freedom Riders"—both blacks and whites—began to travel through Southern states by bus in a nonviolent demand for equal seating on interstate transportation. They were met with bloody violence.

Birmingham, Alabama—often called the most segregated city in the South—took center stage in the spring of 1963. Police brought out attack dogs and high-powered fire hoses to stop civil rights marchers and protesters. Even after an agreement was reached to integrate the city, white racists did not consider the issue to be over.

meantime, he and Alma moved into a house in nearby Phenix City, Alabama.

Powell was assigned to Pathfinder school to take a monthlong advanced Airborne course. He still did not like jumping out of airplanes, though he enjoyed the feeling of floating to earth by parachute.[5]

One night, Powell was hungry and went to buy a hamburger at a drive-in restaurant. Because he was African American, the waitress refused to sell him the

Firefighters in Birmingham aimed their high-pressure hoses at protesters to break up this 1963 civil rights demonstration.

hamburger unless he went around to the back. She said she would pass it to him through the back window. Powell got angry. "I'm not *that* hungry," he said and drove away.[6]

It was still six months before Powell could start his Infantry Officers Advanced Course. So he went to work at the Infantry Board at Fort Benning. His job was to test new weapons and equipment, then recommend which of them the Infantry should buy. It was boring work, but Powell stayed with the job because it meant that he could live at home with Alma and Michael.

In August, Powell became a student once more. It was important to his army career that he take the Infantry Officers Advanced Course. It would take almost a full year, and Powell moved into Fort Benning with his family.

One day during the summer of 1964, Powell returned to the drive-in restaurant that had refused to serve him unless he went to the back window. He again ordered a hamburger. This time he was served from the same window as the white customers. The new president, Lyndon Baines Johnson, had signed into law a bill making racial discrimination illegal in public places such as restaurants, parks, and hotels.

On April 16, 1965, the Powells' daughter, Linda, was born. Colin completed the Infantry Officers Advanced Course a month later. He had the third-highest grade in his class of two hundred students.

In spring 1966, Powell was assigned to teach a course in the same school where he had completed the Infantry Officers Advanced Course. By this time, the United States was actively involved in the war in Vietnam. Its army officers were no longer acting merely as advisers. American troops were fighting the Vietcong and the North Vietnamese who supported them. That meant that the army needed more officers. Powell's job was to train those new officers for combat in Vietnam. He also received another promotion. He was now Major Powell.

Powell returned to school again in August of the following year. This time the army sent him to the United States Army Command and General Staff College in Fort Leavenworth, Kansas. It was there that he learned about the areas of the army besides the infantry. He got a broad, general education about the army. He graduated second in his class in June 1968.

A few weeks later, the army sent Powell back to Vietnam. He did not patrol the jungles of the A Shau Valley this time. He was stationed first at battalion headquarters in Duc Pho and then at American Division headquarters in Chu Lai, on South Vietnam's central coast.

One day in November 1968, Powell was riding in a helicopter near Chu Lai. Other army officers in the helicopter with him included the division commander, Major General Charles Gettys, and the chief of staff. The pilot lost control of the helicopter and its blade hit a tree. The

Powell survived this helicopter wreck in Vietnam
and then pulled his commander to safety.

helicopter fell to the ground, and Powell jumped out just
as smoke began billowing out of the engine. Then he real-
ized that Gettys was hurt and was still inside the helicopter.
Powell ran back and pulled the general to safety.[7] For this
heroic act, Powell received the Soldier's Medal. This is
a medal that the army gives for bravery in noncombat
situations.[8]

Powell did something even more important the next year. A group of army inspectors asked him to look through journals at American Division headquarters to find any unusual entries. He discovered that soldiers led by Lieutenant William Calley Jr. had killed more than two hundred women, children, and old men in the village of My Lai.[9] The incident came to be known as the My Lai massacre and was reported in newspapers and on radio and television stations around the world. The American public was outraged, and the army put a number of men on trial for war crimes.

Before he left Vietnam, Powell received two more medals—the Legion of Merit and the Bronze Star—for outstanding service to his country. He came home from Vietnam in July 1969, an accomplished officer.

Chapter 6

The Yo-Yo Years

 fter Colin Powell returned from Vietnam, he became a graduate student at George Washington University in Washington, D.C. He was there on an army scholarship to get another degree: a master's in business administration (MBA) in data processing. Data processing is the collecting and storing of data—facts and numbers—in a computer, then combining and rearranging that data to get more information from it.

At thirty-two, Powell was the oldest student in most of his classes. It had been eleven years since he last sat in a classroom as a student. He said he found the school work "daunting" and was relieved when he was given an extra six months in which to complete his studies.[1] Powell got A's in all of his courses except one. He got a B in Computer Logic.

The Powells could no longer live on an army base because Colin was not on active duty. They found a house that they liked in Woodbridge, Virginia, in the community of Dale City. The Powells were soon expecting a third child.

In 1971, Powell received his MBA from George Washington University, was promoted to lieutenant colonel, and became the father of a new baby daughter, named Annemarie. Although he was happy to be with his family, he was eager to get back to the army. The army assigned him to work in the Pentagon, just across the Potomac River from Washington, D.C.

The Pentagon, in Arlington, Virginia, is a large office building named for its five-sided shape. It is the headquarters of the Department of Defense, which is in charge of defending the United States against attack from inside or outside the country. The Pentagon employs some twenty thousand military and civilian workers. As a lieutenant colonel in the army, Colin Powell was one of its military employees.

In 1972, the army ordered Powell to apply for a White House Fellowship. That program allows a select group of young Americans to learn firsthand about how the government of the United States is run and to become involved with its top leaders.[2]

Powell left the Pentagon and worked for one year as a White House Fellow in the Office of Management and

In 1971 Powell went to work at the Pentagon,
headquarters of the United States Department of Defense.

Budget (OMB). The OMB assists the president in
developing and carrying out his programs and policies. It
is involved with money, people, laws, and regulations in all
the agencies and programs of the federal government.[3]

Frank Carlucci was deputy director of the OMB at that
time. He had interviewed Powell and hired him to work at
OMB. Not long after this, Carlucci left the agency to
become deputy secretary of the Department of Health,
Education, and Welfare. But he would remain important

in Colin Powell's career, and their paths would cross again many times.

At OMB Powell worked on putting together a document called "A Weekly Compilation of Presidential Directives." For the first time, all the directives, or orders, that the president sent to various government agencies and departments could be found in one place.

Powell worked at OMB from September 1972 until August 1973. A month later, he left Washington to become a battalion commander of troops in South Korea. He had led a platoon of forty soldiers in West Germany. In Korea, he would be in charge of seven hundred soldiers.

Colin Powell arrived in South Korea in September 1973. "Having to leave my wife and children to go off to Korea was, at that point, the most painful thing I had ever faced," he said.[4] But the army did not allow families to go to Korea with its soldiers.

Powell was assigned by the division commander, Major General Henry Emerson, to Camp Casey. The camp was located about twenty-five miles from the demilitarized zone (DMZ). The DMZ is the strip of land dividing North Korea and South Korea. If North Korea attacked the south again, they would do it by coming over the DMZ. The American soldiers were at Camp Casey to help the South Koreans resist any future invasion from the north.

In the meantime, there was very little for the soldiers to do except train and patrol. Many of them spent their time getting into trouble. They lacked discipline, and many used drugs. There was growing tension between African-American and white soldiers.

General Emerson later said that he assigned Powell to Camp Casey because he thought that an African-American soldier might be able to relieve racial tension better than a white soldier could.[5] And that is just what Powell did. He directed the attention of his soldiers away from their physical differences. He told

> "Having to leave my wife and children to go off to Korea was, at that point, the most painful thing I had ever faced."

them, "We're soldiers. Let's remember, that's what pulls us together and let's not let anything put us apart, whether it is racial differences or drugs or anything else."[6]

Emerson was impressed with Powell's ability to command the soldiers, communicate with them, and make them feel good about themselves.[7] He recommended to the army that Powell be promoted as soon as possible.

Powell's tour of duty in South Korea ended in fall 1974. He was sent back to the United States and returned to his old job at the Pentagon. A year later, Powell was accepted into the National War College in Washington, D.C. There he learned about national security issues and how the armed forces would address those security issues. After he graduated, Powell was promoted to full colonel in 1976.

In Korea, Powell's ability to command and motivate his men whipped a difficult, troubled army unit into tiptop shape.

Powell's next assignment was as brigade commander at Fort Campbell, Kentucky. He was put in charge of the 2nd Brigade of the 101st Airborne Division. This time his family could live on the base with him. Powell was happy with his command. In fact, he was hoping to become chief of staff of the 101st Airborne Division when his current assignment was finished.

"Colin was the best brigade commander we had," Major General Jack Wickham said. "He was best in his tactical knowledge, in his feel for soldiers, and his ability to communicate. He had a natural leadership style about him."[8]

While Powell was in Fort Campbell, a new president moved into the White House. Jimmy Carter was inaugurated as America's thirty-ninth president. Carter's national security adviser, Zbigniew Brzezinski, was hiring people to work in the National Security Council.

The National Security Council is composed of the president's senior national security advisers and cabinet members. They meet with the president to advise and assist him in matters of national security and foreign policy.

The Carter Administration had its eye on Colin Powell. He was a perfect candidate for a job with the National Security Council. He was a highly regarded and experienced soldier by then. He had also been a White House Fellow, so he knew his way around the government as well as the battlefield.

The army sent Powell back to Washington, D.C., in February 1977. Brzezinski interviewed him and wanted to hire him to head up the National Security Council's defense program. It was a high-level job. But Powell turned it down, preferring to return to Fort Campbell. He was called back to Washington, D.C., three months later for another interview at the National Security Council. Although he was still not interested in working there, Powell agreed to think about it.

◆◆◆◆◆◆◆◆◆

National Security Adviser

The national security adviser is the head of the National Security Council (NSC). The NSC was created in 1947 to advise the president as to what course of action he should take to keep America safe at home and around the world.

About the same time, he got a call from the Pentagon. He was told that John Kester was looking for someone from the army to become his executive assistant. At that time, John Kester was the assistant to both the Secretary of Defense and the Deputy Secretary of Defense.

Kester had read in an army publication about Powell's background and experience. He saw that Powell had been a White House Fellow, a decorated veteran of the Vietnam and Korean Wars, and had worked at the Pentagon before. The fact that he was African American was also important to the Carter Administration, which wanted to increase opportunities for minorities and women.[9]

Powell went to see Kester. He later recalled the interview as going in part like this:

Powell: "How did you happen to send for me?"

Kester: "I checked you out and I heard a lot of good things."

Powell: "I checked you out, too, and everything I heard was not so good."[10]

Powell's honesty apparently impressed Kester. Powell came away from the interview with yet another high-level job offer.

He returned again to Fort Campbell and finished his assignment there. He was told he was not eligible to become chief of staff of the 101st Airborne. The job required being a helicopter pilot, and Powell was not one.

So he had to decide between the job at the National Security Council and the one at the Department of Defense. When the army ordered him to the Department of Defense, Powell called John Kester and agreed to work at the Pentagon. Then he returned with his family to the Washington, D.C., area.

Powell's job at the Department of Defense was to keep Kester up-to-date on what was going on at the Pentagon, the White House, and in Congress. In 1979 Powell was promoted to brigadier general and transferred to the office of the Deputy Secretary of Defense, Charles Duncan. He would be Duncan's military assistant. Powell, at age forty-two, was now the youngest general in the army.

Maud Powell came to Washington for her son's promotion ceremony, but Luther Powell was too sick to attend. He had been diagnosed with cancer of the liver in 1978.

Neither Duncan nor Powell stayed at the Department of Defense very long. An energy crisis had developed in the United States by that time. Oil was in short supply, so the price of oil had risen, and the American people were very angry about it.

Oil and the Energy Crisis

The United States imports much of the oil it uses for heating its homes and much of the gasoline that runs its cars. Four Middle Eastern countries, Iran, Iraq, Kuwait, and Saudi Arabia, and the South American country of Venezuela got together in 1960 and formed the Organization of Petroleum Exporting Countries (OPEC), which today has twelve member nations. Its purpose was to regulate the amount of oil that was pumped and the price of that oil. The price of oil was relatively low throughout the 1960s.

During the 1970s, OPEC decided that less oil would be pumped than in the past. As a result, the cost of heating oil for homes and businesses and the price of gasoline shot up. With the gas shortage, people across the United States spent hours waiting in line at gas stations to fill up their cars. They wanted their government to do something about the situation. And they wanted a long-term plan that would make the United States less dependent on oil from OPEC and other foreign nations.

The Department of Energy was created to find a variety of reliable and affordable energy sources. In August 1979 Charles Duncan became head of the Department of Energy, and Powell made the move with him. Duncan recognized Powell's intelligence and abilities. At an office party early in 1980 Duncan complimented Powell as "a guy who's going to go all the way."[11]

In November 1980, Ronald Reagan defeated Jimmy Carter, who was running for reelection as president of the United States. President Reagan appointed Caspar Weinberger as Secretary of Defense. Weinberger appointed Frank Carlucci to be Deputy Secretary of Defense. Carlucci again asked Powell to be his military assistant. "Because I'd known him, I knew what talent he had," Carlucci said about his decision.[12] Powell agreed to work for Carlucci.

In less than a year, though, Powell would be able to leave Washington for what he liked best—returning to active duty in the army. In spring 1981, Weinberger appointed Powell assistant commander of the 4th Infantry Division in Fort Carson, Colorado. The Powell family moved west. Michael Powell graduated from high school and spent that summer with his parents in Colorado. In September he went east to begin his freshman year at the College of William and Mary in Virginia.

In spring 1982, Colin Powell was appointed deputy commander of the Army Combined Arms Combat Development Unit at Fort Leavenworth, Kansas.

Chapter 7

Back in Washington

 lthough Colin Powell was happiest in the field as a soldier, his career was about to come to a crossroads. He was being considered for an important job in Washington, D.C. Powell did not want to give up his field command. But he would have to do just that in order to keep his career moving forward. In June 1983, when his Fort Leavenworth assignment was finished, he moved his family back to Washington, D.C.

In July, Caspar Weinberger, the Secretary of Defense, appointed him to be his senior military assistant. Once again Powell went to work at the Pentagon. He was promoted to major general a month later, and a second star was added to the epaulets on the shoulders of his uniform.

Powell attended many meetings in his new job. He came to each one well prepared and was able to speak effectively about the subject at hand. He had learned during his first tour of duty in West Germany that he had the ability to read and remember a lot of facts and information.

This ability was not lost on Caspar Weinberger. He later wrote that one of Powell's assets was that he knew more about the subject matter to be discussed at a

Iran and the United States

For many years, Iran was ruled by a shah, or king, who had a good relationship with the United States. The shah was overthrown in 1979 and replaced by the Ayatollah Ruhollah Khomeini, a Muslim leader. The new government hated the United States because it had supported the shah.

Soon after, President Carter allowed the shah into the U.S. for medical treatment. Iran's leaders were furious and demanded the shah's return. Carter refused. Iranian revolutionaries then took fifty-two Americans hostage in Teheran, intending to exchange the hostages for the shah. Again Carter refused. Instead, the United States stopped buying oil from Iran, and Americans were forbidden to do business with Iran. After more than a year, on the day President Reagan took office, the hostages were finally released. Even so, the United States and Iran remained on bad terms.

meeting than any other person there. He could participate in a meeting effectively because he knew exactly what the meeting was supposed to accomplish.[1]

Powell's job as senior military assistant was also to read materials sent to Weinberger and decide which ones the Secretary of Defense needed to see.

A memo from Robert McFarlane, President Reagan's national security adviser, came into the office in June 1985. It was labeled Top Secret and addressed to both

Leading Up to a Government Scandal

A political group called the Sandinistas had seized power in the Central American country of Nicaragua in 1979. Another group, the *contras*, were fighting to overthrow them. Ronald Reagan did not like the Sandinistas' Communist government. After Reagan became president, the United States began sending help to support the *contras*. Then, in 1984, Congress voted against sending any more money to the *contras*.

In another part of the world, in the Middle Eastern country of Lebanon, terrorists had kidnapped seven Americans and were holding them hostage. These terrorists were on good terms with Iran, a country that was still an enemy of the United States.

These seemingly unrelated situations would lead to a public scandal in the United States government.

Weinberger and Secretary of State George Shultz. The subject was the United States policy toward Iran. The boycott of Iran was still in effect, and the memo proposed ways for the United States to improve relations with Iran. The suggestions included selling Iran some military equipment.

Powell thought the plan was "audacious." The United States considered Iran a terrorist state, and President Reagan had promised never to deal with terrorists. Powell passed the memo along to his boss, who called it "almost too absurd to comment on."[2]

But the proposal continued to circulate in Washington, D.C. The families of the kidnapped Americans held in Lebanon spoke to President Reagan. They asked him to do everything in his power to free their loved ones. Reagan and his advisers thought that Iran would help free the hostages in exchange for the military equipment. The United States could not openly do business with Iran, so the equipment was sold to Iran secretly and indirectly.

At Weinberger's request, Powell transferred 4,508 TOW missiles from the army to the Central Intelligence Agency (CIA). This was legal under a law called the Economy Act, which allows one government agency to sell goods and services to another to avoid duplication.[3] The CIA then sold the missiles to an intermediary, who sold them to Iran. The Iranians were supposed to persuade the terrorists in Lebanon to release their American hostages. In the end, only three of the seven hostages were freed, and three more Americans were kidnapped.

In the second secret deal, money from the sale of the weapons was sent to the rebels in Nicaragua. This was illegal because Congress had ruled against U.S. support of the *contras*. The scandal that followed the discovery of all these secret deals became known as the Iran-*contra* affair.

> Powell did not think the United States should sell weapons to Iran.

An investigation of the Iran-*contra* affair began in 1986. Investigators spoke to anyone in the government who might have known something about it. They questioned the president, the vice president, members of the CIA, the State Department, and the Department of Defense, including Colin Powell.

Weinberger came to Powell's defense. He confirmed that General Powell had carried out his orders to transfer army weapons to the CIA. But he denied that there was any link between Powell and the Nicaraguan *contras*.[4]

By the time of the Iran-*contra* investigation, Powell had already left the Pentagon. He had been promoted to three-star general and returned to the army. In June 1986, he was sent to West Germany for the second time in his career. Later, when called back to Washington, D.C., to tell investigators what he knew about the Iran-*contra* affair, Powell would be cleared of any wrongdoing.

Alma and their daughters went to West Germany with Powell. They were met there by Michael Powell, who had graduated from college, enlisted in the army, and been stationed in West Germany.

Some things had changed in West Germany since Colin Powell's first time there. The Berlin Wall had been built in 1961, dividing the city of Berlin in half. The western part of the city was controlled by the United States and its allies. The eastern half was controlled by the Soviet Union. Powell's job was the same as it had been during his earlier tour of duty—to stop the Soviet army from crossing the border into West Germany. But now he was commanding seventy-two thousand American soldiers.

By that time McFarlane and his successor as national security adviser, John Poindexter, had resigned. Frank Carlucci was appointed national security adviser to President Ronald Reagan.

The National Security Council was in trouble because of the Iran-*contra* affair. The American people had lost faith in the council's ability to advise the president about matters of security. Carlucci's job was to restore America's faith in the National Security Council.

One day Colin Powell received a telephone call from Frank Carlucci. "I want you to be my deputy," Carlucci told Powell.[5] He said later that he chose Powell "because he was the best, most talented person I knew" for the job.[6]

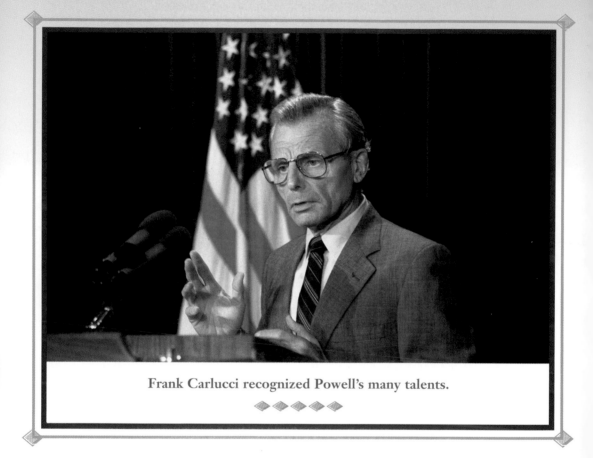

Frank Carlucci recognized Powell's many talents.

Powell was afraid that taking the job would put an end to his army career. It would mean giving up his current command after only five months. That was not enough time to earn him another promotion and a fourth star. So he turned down Carlucci's offer. Carlucci called him again to urge him to reconsider, and Powell turned the job down again. "I gave him every reason I could think of," he said.[7] Carlucci persisted until Powell said he would take the job only if President Reagan asked him to do it. So Carlucci asked the president to call Powell.

The president of the United States is also commander-in-chief of all the armed forces of the United States. That meant he was Powell's boss. As a soldier, Powell had to follow orders given by his commander-in-chief. Powell accepted the job as deputy national security adviser and returned to Washington, D.C.

Powell started his new job early in 1987. The Iran-*contra* affair investigators had recommended changes that the National Security Council needed to make. These included not making any more secret deals like selling weapons to enemy countries.

Powell's job was to put those changes into effect. "I was hired by Frank Carlucci in the first instance to help reestablish confidence . . . in the NSC system and . . . to fix something which, at that time, was seen to be broken," he explained.[8] Powell was the perfect person for the job. He had a proven ability to make things happen. He was likable, conducted meetings well, and could persuade people to do what needed to get done.[9]

In June 1987, Michael Powell, the Powells' son, was in an accident in Germany. He and two other soldiers were driving in an army jeep. As the driver began to fall asleep at the wheel, the jeep drifted into a lane of oncoming traffic. Suddenly, the driver turned the wheel abruptly to avoid a truck that was coming toward them. He lost control and the jeep rolled over. Michael was thrown out of the jeep, which then landed on top of him. Michael was so badly hurt that doctors thought he would surely die.

Colin and Alma Powell flew to West Germany to be with their son. Colin Powell saw to it that his son received the best possible care. Michael was soon transferred to Walter Reed Army Medical Center in Washington, D.C. His mother stayed with him around the clock. His father visited him at the hospital every day.

General Powell, with his wife at his side, gives a farewell salute as he leaves his army field command in West Germany in December 1986.

Michael Powell did not die. During the next year, he had several operations. While he was in the hospital, Jane Knott, a woman he had dated in college, began visiting him. Jane and Michael fell in love. When he was well again, Michael retired from the army and took a job with the Department of Defense. Jane and Michael married in October 1988.

While Michael Powell was in the hospital, things were changing in Washington, D.C. Caspar Weinberger had resigned from his position as Secretary of Defense. Frank Carlucci was appointed to the job. Colin Powell was promoted to national security adviser. He had taken Carlucci's place at meetings many times. President Reagan knew Powell and respected his judgment.[10]

One of Powell's first assignments as national security adviser was to plan and arrange a meeting between President Reagan and the president of the Soviet Union, Mikhail Gorbachev. The two leaders met in Washington, D.C., in December 1988 to sign an agreement eliminating all medium-range missiles.

Just a month earlier, George H. W. Bush, vice president under Ronald Reagan, had been elected to be the next president of the United States. When Bush took office on January 20, 1989, he would appoint his own national security adviser. So, after just a year on the job, it was time for Powell to decide what he wanted to do next.

U.S. National Security Adviser Colin Powell
answers questions from reporters.

The president-elect offered Powell several positions in the incoming administration. Did he want to become director of the Central Intelligence Agency? Would deputy director of the Department of State suit him better? Or would he prefer to stay on as national security adviser until a new one was appointed?

Once again, as he had in 1971 and 1980, Powell preferred to return to the army as soon as possible. He turned down all of the president-elect's offers. In February he was sent to Forces Command at Fort McPherson, which is near Atlanta, Georgia. He received a promotion to four-star general. Now his command included about one million troops—active duty soldiers, reservists, and Special Forces, or Green Berets.

A news conference was called to announce Powell's new assignment. Reagan's spokesman, Marlin Fitzwater, told reporters that Reagan "has the highest respect and affection for General Powell."[11]

But that assignment would not last long either.

In 1989, Powell became the top-ranked
military officer in the United States.

Chapter 8

Chairman of the Joint Chiefs of Staff

n August 1989, Colin Powell was called to the Pentagon in Washington, D.C., to meet with Secretary of Defense Richard Cheney. Powell was Cheney's top choice for chairman of the Joint Chiefs of Staff.[1] He had the right experience for the job. He had worked both in the Pentagon and in the White House. He had adequate military experience. Cheney said he would recommend that President Bush appoint Powell to the position if Powell wanted the job.

Powell did not really want to accept. He was already doing the job that made him happy: being a soldier. But the president was his commander-in-chief. So he told the Defense Secretary, "If you and the President want me, I'll take it and do my best."[2] Calling him "a complete soldier,"

President Bush nominated Powell in August 1989.[3] "He will bring leadership, initiative and wisdom to our efforts to keep our military forces strong and ready," the president said when he announced the nomination.[4] The Senate confirmed the nomination on September 20, 1989. Colin Powell became the youngest person, and first African American, to be named chairman of the Joint Chiefs of Staff.

Powell was well aware that he was making history. He said in a speech to the National Association of Black Journalists that his appointment as chairman of the Joint

The Joint Chiefs of Staff

The Joint Chiefs of Staff is composed of the top officers in the army, the navy, the air force, and the marines. Its chairman is the highest-ranking military officer in the United States.

Together the Joint Chiefs carry out the president's orders by developing military plans for the United States. The chairman of the Joint Chiefs of Staff is the link between the military and the civilian government. He tells the Joint Chiefs about the president's plans for the military. Then he briefs the president about how the plans are being carried out. He is the president's chief military adviser. He also advises the National Security Council and the Secretary of Defense.

Chiefs of Staff "never would have been possible without the sacrifices of those black soldiers who served this great nation in war for nearly 300 years previously."[5]

A public swearing-in ceremony was scheduled to take place on October 3. It was to be held outdoors on the grounds of the Pentagon. Powell's family would be seated in the front row as honored guests. His sister, Marilyn, and her husband were expected to attend. His childhood friend from the Bronx, Gene Norman, and his wife also were invited.

> "He will bring leadership, initiative and wisdom to our efforts to keep our military forces strong and ready."

As it turned out, Powell began his new job even before he was sworn in. He received word on October 1 that rebels in Panama planned to overthrow the government of Manuel Noriega. The rebels were asking the United States for help with their coup. Powell, Cheney, and a few other high-level government officials briefed the president at the White House about the situation in Panama. President George H. W. Bush wanted to see Noriega out of power. Noriega was a dictator who treated his people harshly. He was accused of being a drug dealer as well.

Powell's advice to the president, however, was that the United States should wait and see what happened with the rebels in Panama.[6] He did not think it was the right

The Joint Chiefs of Staff in 1989,
with their chairman, General Colin Powell.

time for the United States to intervene. He wanted to be sure Noriega's rule would be replaced by a democracy. It was good advice because the rebels were disorganized and failed in their coup. Powell continued to keep a close eye on Panama.

The public swearing-in ceremony took place as scheduled on October 3. Powell moved his family into Quarters 6 in Fort Myer, Virginia. Quarters 6 is the official home of the chairman of the Joint Chiefs of Staff, just as the White House is the home of the president of the United States.

The world situation began changing almost as soon as Powell was sworn in as chairman. The Berlin Wall came down in Germany. People living in East Germany were no longer separated from those living in West Germany.

In November President Corazon Aquino of the Philippines asked the United States to send troops to put down a rebel group that was trying to oust her government. She said that her palace had been bombed by rebel airplanes.

Powell briefed President Bush on a plan proposed by the Joint Chiefs to help the Philippine president. The United States would keep the rebel airplanes on the ground. Any rebel craft that got into the air would be shot down. A few United States planes flew over Philippine airfields. The rebels were intimidated and gave up almost immediately.

There was more talk that the rebels in Panama would try again to overthrow Manuel Noriega's government. In December an American Marine stationed in Panama was shot and killed. A navy officer and his wife were taken prisoner. Now American lives were in danger in Panama. The time to send more troops into Panama was drawing closer.

The invasion of Panama began a few days later, on December 20, 1989. It was called Operation Just Cause, and it lasted about ten days. "We will chase him, and we will find

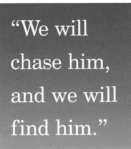

"We will chase him, and we will find him."

him," Powell said about Manuel Noriega as Operation Just Cause began.[7]

Noriega was not captured. Instead, he surrendered on January 3, 1990. He was arrested and brought to the United States. After being tried and convicted on drug charges, he was sent to an American prison to serve a forty-year sentence.

United States troops were again involved in a war a year later. This time they were sent to Kuwait, a country on the Persian Gulf in southwest Asia, to drive out invading

Manuel Noriega of Panama.

Iraq Invades Kuwait

In August 1990, Iraqi president Saddam Hussein invaded the oil-rich country of Kuwait. Saudi Arabia, a neighboring country, asked the United States for protection in case Iraq invaded Saudi Arabia next.

Saudi Arabia is a major oil-producing country. A great deal of its oil is imported into the United States to heat American homes and businesses and to fuel its cars and trucks. It would not be good for the United States if Iraq invaded Saudi Arabia and stopped it from exporting its oil. So President Bush sent 230,000 American troops to protect Saudi Arabia's border with Iraq. This military operation was called Desert Shield.

In November 1990 the United Nations Security Council gave Saddam Hussein an ultimatum. He was told to withdraw his troops from Kuwait by January 15, 1991. But January 15 passed and the Iraqi troops were still in Kuwait. President Bush won approval in Congress on January 16 to begin a military assault on Iraq to get its troops out of Kuwait. Operation Desert Shield became Operation Desert Storm. If Iraq did not get out of Kuwait on its own, the United States would force Iraq to withdraw from Kuwait.

> "If you are going to commit the armed forces of the U.S. to a military operation that could involve conflict, and loss of life, then do it right."

Iraqi forces. Powell approved of Operation Desert Storm. But he wanted it to be "massive and swift, not gradual."[8] He said, "If you are going to commit the armed forces of the U.S. to a military operation that could involve conflict, and loss of life, then do it right."[9] And doing it right meant having a clear objective, sending in a huge military force, achieving that objective, and getting out quickly.

The United Nations Security Council's deadline came and went. Iraqi troops remained in Kuwait. In February, President Bush ordered American troops into combat. They were joined by troops from England, France, Saudi Arabia, Egypt, Syria, and other nations.

Saddam Hussein's forces were defeated after six weeks of aerial bombing and four days of ground combat. They fled from Kuwait. But that would not be the end of hostilities between Saddam Hussein and the United States. War between those two nations would erupt again more than a decade later.

As a result of Operation Desert Storm, Colin Powell became a national hero. President Bush reappointed him in 1991 to a second term as chairman of the Joint Chiefs.

General Powell's "massive and swift"
Operation Desert Storm made him a national hero.

> Many people thought Powell would make a good vice president.

His name and photograph appeared in many magazines and newspapers. He was interviewed on TV news programs. But he did not like being in the public eye. He preferred being at home with his family. Michael was now a law student at Georgetown University; Linda was a television actress; and Annemarie was in her junior year at the College of William and Mary.

Still, talk around Washington, D.C., was about nominating Colin Powell as a vice-presidential candidate when the president ran for a second term in 1992. But Powell said he did not want the job. He preferred to remain in his current position as chairman of the Joint Chiefs of Staff.

And stay he did. Bill Clinton defeated George H. W. Bush in the 1992 election. But before the new president was inaugurated and before Powell's second term as chairman of the Joint Chiefs was over, Powell still had important work to do.

A civil war was going on in Somalia, a country in East Africa, and there had been a long drought. There was no rainfall to water the crops and grow grass for cattle to eat. Hundreds of thousands of people had no food and were dying of starvation. After the 1992 election, the United States began Operation Restore Hope in Somalia. It flew vast amounts of food into the country and sent in troops

President H. W. Bush, left, praised Powell's leadership
in the invasion of Panama and the war against Iraq.

> "I had found something to do with my life . . . that I loved doing."

to make sure that the food was distributed to the people who needed it.

On the day before Thanksgiving 1992, Colin Powell briefed the president on how this humanitarian effort would be carried out. It took 25,400 troops to do the job, but Operation Restore Hope was a success. It achieved its objective of feeding the starving Somali people.

In summer 1993, Powell's second term as chairman of the Joint Chiefs of Staff came to an end. That fall he retired from the army after thirty-five years of service. He had achieved the highest commissioned rank in the armed forces. Now he wanted to go home and write his autobiography. He also had offers to give speeches and serve on the board of directors of some corporations and was considering them.

Powell's retirement ceremony was held outdoors in Fort Myer. His family, relatives, and many old friends watched the ceremony. Troops paraded and jet planes and helicopters flew overhead. President Clinton presented Powell with the Presidential Medal of Freedom, the nation's highest nonmilitary award.

Powell later summarized his army career: "I had found something to do with my life that was honorable and useful, that I could do well, and that I loved doing," he wrote.[10] Now Colin Powell was without a job.

At Powell's retirement ceremony in 1993,
President Clinton, right, thanked him for a job well done.

Chapter 9

Private
Citizen

 olin Powell was a private citizen once again. He and Alma moved into a house in McLean, Virginia, a suburb of Washington, D.C. Since he had traveled so much during his career, Powell was now content to stay at home. "Having seen so much of the world and having lived on planes for years, I am no longer much interested in travel," he wrote.[1]

He began to write his autobiography and accepted speaking invitations from organizations and schools. But mostly he stayed at home and tinkered with the old Volvo cars he loved to restore.

In December 1993 he and Alma flew to London, where Colin was knighted by the Queen of England. Colin Powell of Kelly Street in the Bronx became a Knight Commander of the Order of Bath.

Powell, here with his wife, Alma, was honored by Queen Elizabeth II
with the second highest award for a foreigner in Britain.

Haiti

Haiti is a country in the West Indies, located on the western third of the island of Hispaniola. It lies in the Caribbean Sea, between Cuba and Puerto Rico. Most of its citizens are poor farmers who raise crops and small animals to feed themselves and their families.

In the past, Haiti has been ruled by a series of dictators who often used violence against their people. In 1964, Francois Duvalier declared himself president for life. He appointed his son, Jean-Claude, to rule Haiti after he died. Both Duvaliers used the army and the secret police to make sure that all their harsh policies were carried out.

Other dictators followed until 1990, when Haitians elected Jean-Bertrand Aristide president. Some rebel army leaders threw Aristide out of office a year later, forcing him to leave the country.

In 1993, under pressure from many countries, including the United States, the rebels agreed to give up and allow Aristide to return to Haiti as its president. Then they changed their minds. In September 1994, the United States started sending soldiers to Haiti, ready to force rebels out of power. Could the situation be resolved without fighting?

The United States did not forget about Powell. At President Clinton's request, Powell was part of a group of Americans who traveled to South Africa in May 1994. They witnessed Nelson Mandela's inauguration as the first black president of South Africa. Four months later Powell went to Haiti on a peacekeeping mission with former president Jimmy Carter.

The United States was ready to invade that Caribbean island. Three days before the fighting was to begin, the Carter group landed in Haiti. Their purpose was to persuade the rebels to give up peacefully, leave the island, and restore Jean-Bertrand Aristide to his position as president. With just six hours to go before the invasion, an agreement was signed handing the government back to Aristide. The invasion did not take place.

Powell considered the trip a success. "Because of what we accomplished, young Americans, and probably far more Haitians, who would have died were still alive," he wrote.[2]

As 1994 drew to a close, President Clinton called Powell to a meeting at the White House. Would Powell like to take over the job of secretary of state, replacing Warren Christopher, who wanted to quit? Powell declined the offer. He explained that he needed more time out of

> Even after he retired, Powell was called upon to travel and represent the United States in foreign affairs.

public office. He was writing his autobiography, making speeches, and just enjoying his new role as a private citizen. "If the nation had faced an immediate crisis, it would have been impossible to say no," he wrote later.[3]

Powell finished writing his autobiography, *My American Journey*, and went on a national speaking tour to promote it. It seemed as if his service to his country had ended and that he would remain a private citizen. But that was not to be.

> Next, would Powell be running for president?

At the first stop on the book tour, a McLean bookstore near the Powell home, about two thousand people waited in line to buy Powell's book and have him autograph it. The crowds were large at every stop on the four-week tour, which took Powell to twenty-six cities. At every stop, people asked him whether he would be a candidate for president of the United States in 1996.

The news media was asking Powell that very same question. "I have to think about it," he told one interviewer. "I care very deeply about this country and over the last two years a large number of people have spoken to me as I've traveled around the country and asked me to consider it. So, I am considering it."[4]

And consider it he did. For two months people wondered: Would he or would he not become the first African-American presidential candidate? On November 8, 1995, Powell held a news conference to announce

On his book tour in 1995,
Powell signed autographs for his many fans.

his decision. He would *not* run for president of the United States in 1996. He told his audience that being a candidate required a commitment and passion for political life that he did not feel, unlike "the kind of passion and the kind of commitment that I felt every day of my 35 years as a soldier."[5] But he did have plans for his future. "I will give my talent and energy to charitable and educational activities," he explained.[6] He joined the board of trustees of the Boys and Girls Clubs of America and the Children's Health Fund. In January 1996 he was named to the board

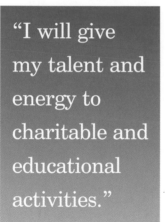

"I will give my talent and energy to charitable and educational activities."

of trustees at Howard University, a prestigious college for African-American students. The primary job of board members is to raise money for their organizations and to decide how that money is to be spent.

Many people questioned the reason for Powell's decision not to run for president. Some thought Alma Powell had convinced her husband not to run because she was concerned for his safety. When a reporter asked her whether that was the reason, she replied, "I think everybody has known that I have had a concern, but I want you to know that it certainly played no part in his decision."[7]

In August 1996 the Republican National Convention was held in San Diego, California. The Republicans nominated Senator Robert Dole as their candidate for president of the United States. They invited Colin Powell to address the convention. In his speech, covered live on television, Powell told the audience why he believed that Dole should become the next president of the United States. "He is a man of strength, maturity, and integrity. He is a man who can bring trust back to government and bring Americans together again."[8] Senator Dole was up against President Clinton, who was running for a second term. On Election Day in November, President Clinton was reelected.

Powell resumed traveling around the country talking to people about his autobiography and the issues that concerned them. He continued to raise money for the children's charities and the schools that he favored. He became a much-requested speaker, receiving as much as $60,000 for a speech.

In April 1997, he joined President Clinton and former presidents George H. W. Bush, Jimmy Carter, and Gerald Ford in Philadelphia for a three-day conference on volunteering. The purpose of the conference was to get more people interested in volunteering as advisers for disadvantaged children and for businesses to donate money for children's health and education. He told those in attendance that disadvantaged children "are at risk of growing up unskilled, unlearned or, even worse, unloved."[9] The initial goal was to help 2 million children by the year 2000. As a result of the conference, an organization called

Living by the Rules

Powell's integrity and common-sense wisdom are reflected in his well-known 13 Rules to Live By. They include advice such as "GET MAD, THEN GET OVER IT." "SHARE CREDIT." "IT CAN BE DONE!" "HAVE A VISION. BE DEMANDING." "REMAIN CALM. BE KIND." He placed these statements in his office as reminders to himself and as advice to others. Powell personalized his office to reflect his interests. His varied musical tastes run from Carly Simon to Benny Goodman, from Louis Armstrong to Mozart. Among the mementos on his desk were a brass model of a 1927 Volvo, a doorknob from Morris High School, and a chunk of the former Berlin Wall.

America's Promise—the Alliance for Youth was started. Powell was appointed its chairman. The name America's Promise refers to five promises that every child in the country deserves: (1) Caring adults in their lives, such as parents, teachers, coaches, friends; (2) a safe environment after school; (3) a healthy start in life; (4) the opportunity to learn marketable skills; and (5) the chance to experience the satisfaction of volunteering and helping others.

Powell spoke to groups of teachers and school administrators and urged them to set a good example for their students to follow. "Children sometimes listen to you and your lectures. But they're really watching your actions. If they see people doing the right thing, people who are always optimistic and trying to improve themselves, they'll want to follow in their directions," he said at a conference in Washington, D.C.[10]

The question of his running for president would not go away. Wherever Powell appeared, reporters and ordinary people turned out in great numbers to see him. When he was on television to talk about volunteering, he was asked whether he intended to run for president in the year 2000. He told everyone that he would not be a candidate but acknowledged, "If it [the question of my candidacy] wasn't there, then I wouldn't get as much attention that allows me to talk about volunteerism."[11]

As the twentieth century drew to a close, the American people were still wondering: Would Colin Powell run for the highest office in the land?

Chapter 10

Another Return to Public Service

olin Powell had been a four-star general in the United States Army. He had served in Washington, D.C., as the country's National Security Advisor and then as the Chairman of the Joint Chiefs of Staff. He was respected and liked by those who knew him. People thought that he would make a good candidate for president of the United States.

But, as he had four years earlier, Powell again said that he would not be a candidate for president of the United States. In spring 2000, Powell visited Texas governor George W. Bush at his Texas ranch. Governor Bush—son of former president George H. W. Bush—had announced that he wanted to be the Republican candidate for president of the United States. Reporters asked Powell whether he wanted to become Bush's running mate. Powell replied quite firmly, "I do not seek elective office, and so I am not a candidate for the vice presidency."[1]

When rumors began circulating that Bush, if elected, was considering appointing Colin Powell to a position in his Cabinet, Powell showed more flexibility. "In any other capacity, one has to listen when a president asks you to consider a job," he said.[2]

Meanwhile he attended the Republican National Convention in Philadelphia in late July. The Republicans there nominated George W. Bush as their candidate for president. They asked Powell to speak at the convention.

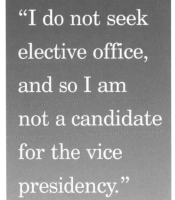

"I do not seek elective office, and so I am not a candidate for the vice presidency."

"Governor Bush has rightly made children and education the centerpiece of his campaign for president," Powell said in his speech to the delegates at the convention. "Every child deserves and must receive a quality education."[3] Powell also spoke about the need to give minority citizens more opportunities to achieve success. "The [Republican] party must follow the governor's lead in reaching out to minority communities, and particularly the African-American community, and not just during an election year campaign."[4]

Powell's speech to the delegates, carried on national television, was important because it touched on two key issues of George W. Bush's campaign—education and minority inclusion.

Soon after the convention, word got around that if he became president, George W. Bush would ask Powell to be his secretary of state. Reporters hounded Powell for an answer. Would he accept the position if it were offered to him? "I have not yet been asked, and if that question would be posed to me, I think I should answer it directly to the governor at that time before answering it to anyone else," he told them.[5]

News spread even before the election that presidential candidate George W. Bush wanted General Powell to be a central part of his team as U.S. Secretary of State.

Election Day came and the voters went to the polls. The Democratic candidate, Al Gore, had an edge in the popular vote, but the Electoral College numbers were very close. Because of the controversy over counting the votes in the state of Florida, many weeks passed before it was announced that George W. Bush would be the next president.

On December 16, Powell stood next to George W. Bush as the president-elect announced to the nation that Colin Powell was his choice to be secretary of state. Bush blinked back tears as he called Powell "an American hero."[6]

The Electoral College

Americans vote for the candidate of their choice, but they do not elect the president directly. That is done by the Electoral College, which is made up of a group of delegates from each state, called electors. The voters in each state tell these electors which candidate to vote for. They do this by their votes on Election Day, called the popular vote. The candidate who wins the popular vote in a state gets all the electoral votes in that state.

Next Powell went to Washington, D.C., for his interview with members of the Senate Foreign Relations Committee. Powell told the senators that he believed in a strong North Atlantic Treaty Organization (NATO), to which the United States and many European countries belong. He said he hoped to work with America's friends and allies to form new relationships with countries such as China, Russia, and North Korea. Like the president-elect, he wanted to move forward on the issue of arms control with Russia. Both countries would get rid of their weapons of mass destruction. And, he said, he agreed with George W. Bush's idea to build a national missile defense system to protect the United States from long-range missiles fired by another country.

Speaking about the situation in Iraq, Powell said,

Standing between George and Laura Bush,
Colin Powell accepts the nomination to be secretary of state.

"This is the tenth year anniversary of the beginning of Desert Storm, a war we wish we didn't have to fight. Unfortunately, Saddam Hussein is still in power."[7] It would turn out to be unfinished business.

Powell later said that he saw his primary mission at that time as being one of helping the president strengthen relations with countries around the world, dealing with crises that they knew would come along, and giving the president the best advice he could.[8]

With the Foreign Relations Committee's recommendation and the full Senate's confirmation, Colin Powell became the nation's first African-American secretary of state. Powell started his new job on January 22, 2001. Three weeks later he made his first trip to a foreign country as secretary of state. He went to Mexico with President Bush to meet with the president of Mexico. They talked about cooperation between the two countries. The issues included the illegal migration of Mexicans to the United States and prosperity, or wealth, for the countries on both sides of the border.

A week later Powell was in the Middle East and in Europe, talking to leaders about the problems in the Middle East. Palestinian suicide bombers were entering Israel and killing themselves and Israelis. Israel was retaliating by bulldozing the homes of suspected suicide bombers and building homes for Israeli settlers in Palestinian neighborhoods. "When you start knocking down buildings with bulldozers, don't expect people not to respond to this kind of activity," Powell said later that year.[9] Both Israel and the Palestinians were caught up in a vicious circle of violence.

By the end of 2001, the new secretary of state had visited more than thirty-five countries in North America, the Middle East, Europe, South America, and the Far East.

In 2002 Powell continued to travel. He made sixteen trips overseas, visiting forty-one countries. At each stop he explained the United States' position on issues of mutual interest. In May 2002, he went to Reykjavik, Iceland, for a NATO meeting. He spoke to the foreign ministers there about the United States' desire to see new countries admitted to NATO. He also urged the forging of new relationships between NATO and Russia, the Ukraine, and other countries.

Powell addressed the United Nations Security Council on September 11, 2002. It was the first anniversary of the tragic events of exactly a year before. On September 11, 2001, terrorists had flown hijacked airplanes into the World Trade Center in New York City, the Pentagon in Washington, D.C., and a field in Pennsylvania. Thousands of innocent people had been killed. Powell told the delegates at the United Nations, "The attacks on our soil drew us closer as a people. They also drew us closer to people of kindness and good will across the globe."[10]

Secretary of State Colin Powell, center, and foreign ministers at a North American Treaty Organization (NATO) meeting in Iceland. Powell saw building strong foreign relations as a top priority.

There was also the issue of what to do about Iraqi dictator Saddam Hussein. Many people thought he should have been removed from office during Operation Desert Storm. Now word came from the U.S. Central Intelligence Agency (CIA) that Iraq had weapons of mass destruction. "The intelligence case is clear, that they have weapons of mass destruction . . . and they are trying to develop more," Powell said.[11] These weapons could kill thousands of people at one time.

In late November 2002, President Bush asked the United Nations Security Council to send troops into Iraq to force Saddam Hussein to get rid of his weapons of mass destruction. The council refused the president's request. Many members were not sure that Iraq still had any such weapons and wanted proof that they existed. The U.N. sent an inspection team to Iraq to search for the weapons.

Powell advised the president not to send U.S. troops into Iraq until the inspectors had finished their work. The disagreement between Powell and the president was reported in newspapers and on television.

President Bush and his main ally, Great Britain's prime minister, Tony Blair, insisted that the weapons existed and were a serious threat to world peace. They wanted to send troops to Iraq to remove Saddam Hussein from office and to rid Iraq of its weapons of mass destruction. The president was not happy that his secretary of state had disagreed with him publicly. A coolness developed between the men.

Still, the year 2003 again found Powell on the go. He made ten separate trips to Europe as well as trips to Asia, South America, the Middle East, and Africa. He attended the World Economic Forum in Switzerland in January. He met there with civic, government, and business leaders from all over the globe. He told them what the United States and its allies were doing to stop terrorism in countries around the world. He said that U.S. troops were in Afghanistan to find Osama bin Laden, the terrorist behind the World Trade Center bombing. "And as soon as our troops are needed no longer, they will depart," he promised.[12]

He told the delegates that the United States was building trust around the world. "Afghanistan's leaders and Afghanistan's people know that they can trust America to do this, to do the right thing," he said about the United States presence in Afghanistan.[13] He named other places in the world where the United States was trying to build trust. They included Africa, Bosnia, Korsovo, and Latin America. And he appealed to the members to back the United States if it decided to go to war with Iraq.

On February 5, 2003, Powell appeared before the United Nations Security Council again. He talked about Resolution 1441, which the council had passed in November 2002. Resolution 1441 gave Iraq one last chance to get rid of its weapons of mass destruction. Now, Powell told the Security Council, intelligence sources said that Iraq still had weapons of mass destruction. He asked the Security Council to enforce Resolution 1441. But the United Nations still took no action. On March 19, 2003, the United States and its allies invaded Iraq.

Powell had a personal problem to worry about, too. In September, he went to the doctor for a physical checkup. Tests showed that he had cancer in his prostate gland, a small organ that is part of the male reproductive system. There are several ways to treat prostate cancer. Powell chose to have his entire prostate gland removed. On December 15, Powell entered Walter Reed Army Medical Center in Washington, D.C., to have the prostate surgery.

It was successful, and he was able to return to work within a few weeks.

Soon he was traveling around the world again. In January 2004 he went to Mexico and then to Georgia, a country on the edge of the Black Sea, for the inauguration of its first president. Georgia had once been part of the Soviet Union. Now it was an independent nation. Powell also went to Russia to talk with its president. As January drew to a close, Powell was back in the United States.

A short time later, Powell was back on the road, going to Europe, Asia, and the Middle East. He met several times with Israeli and Palestinian leaders to promote President Bush's dream of having Israelis and Palestinians living as neighbors in peace and security.

On November 2, 2004, Americans again went to the polls to elect a president. This time, President Bush ran against John Kerry, a senator from Massachusetts. Bush was elected to a second term.

Ten days after the election, Colin Powell sent a letter of resignation to the president. In it, he said that it was time for him to step down as secretary of state and return to private life. President George W. Bush accepted Powell's resignation. Powell would continue in his role as secretary of state until late January 2005, when Condoleeza Rice, the next secretary of state, would take over.

Powell traveled to Indonesia on January 5, 2005, on behalf of the United States. He was overwhelmed by the

Powell's career has taken him from soldier to statesman.
What will be next?

catastrophic destruction and loss of life caused by the tsunami that had hit Southeast Asia in December 2004. "I've been in war, and I've been through a number of hurricanes, tornadoes and other relief operations, but I have never seen anything like this," he said.[14]

On January 12, the White House announced that after a two-year search, no weapons of mass destruction had been found in Iraq. President Bush appointed a committee to investigate why the previous intelligence had been wrong. However, the president had no doubts about the war in Iraq.

Powell expressed "regret" about the incorrect intelligence as to "actual stockpiles of weapons." But, he said, there was "no question that we were correct with respect to the nature of the regime of Saddam Hussein, the fact that he'd used such weapons in the past, that he had the intention to have them again, and he had the capability to have them again."[15]

A few days later, on January 19, Powell said an emotional good-bye to the staff of the State Department. Powell had served his country as a soldier and as a statesman. In his army career, he rose to the highest military position in the nation. As a civilian, he became one of the most popular secretaries of state in history, admired both in the United States and around the world. After forty-six years of public service, Colin Powell was now free to decide what he wanted to do for the rest of his life.

Chronology

1937—Colin Luther Powell born in Harlem, New York City, on April 5.

1954—Enters City College of New York; joins Reserve Officer Training Corps (ROTC).

1958—Graduates from college with degree in geology and an honor in ROTC; enters the army as a second lieutenant; sent to Fort Benning, Georgia, for training.

1959—Sent to West Germany for first field command; promoted to first lieutenant.

1962—Marries Alma Johnson; sent to Fort Bragg, North Carolina, for more training, then to Vietnam.

1963—Son Michael born; returns to Fort Benning, Georgia, for advanced officer training.

1965—Daughter Linda born.

1968—Sent to Vietnam for second time.

1969—Returns to Washington, D.C.; enters George Washington University as graduate student to study data processing.

1971—Daughter Annemarie born; earns master's degree in business administration; goes to work at the Pentagon in Arlington, Virginia; promoted to lieutenant colonel.

1972—Becomes a White House Fellow; works at the Office of Management and Budget.

1973—Sent to South Korea as battalion commander.

1975—Enters National War College in Washington, D.C.

1976—Promoted to colonel; sent to Fort Campbell, Kentucky, to command the 2nd Brigade of the 101st Airborne Division.

1979—Becomes military assistant to deputy secretary of defense in Washington, D.C.; promoted to brigadier general.

1983—Becomes senior military assistant to secretary of defense; promoted to major general.

1986—Sent to West Germany for a second time; promoted to lieutenant general.

1987—Returns to Washington, D.C., as deputy national security adviser; later becomes national security adviser.

1989—Sent to Forces Command at Fort McPherson, Georgia; promoted to four-star general; returns to Washington, D.C., to become chairman of the Joint Chiefs of Staff.

1993—Retires from army.

1995—*My American Journey*, Powell's autobiography, is published.

2001—Becomes secretary of state.

2004—Resigns as secretary of state.

Chapter Notes

Chapter 1. The Long Wait Ends

1. Author interview with Colin Powell, January 2, 2004.
2. Ibid.
3. "Remarks at Announcement of Powell's Nomination," *The New York Times*, December 17, 2000, p. 51.
4. Ibid.
5. Jane Perlez, "Softball for Powell and With No Sweat," *The New York Times*, January 18, 2001, p. A17.
6. "Confirmation Hearing by Colin L. Powell," *U.S. Department of State website*, January 17, 2001, <http://www.state.gov/secretary/rm/2001/443pf.htm> (April 21, 2003).

Chapter 2. A Childhood of Love, Learning, and Discipline

1. Christopher P. Baker, *Jamaica* (Victoria, Australia: Lonely Planet Publications, 2003), p. 14.
2. Ibid., p. 16.
3. Ken Adelman, "What I've Learned: Ground Zero: Colin Powell on War, Peace, and Balancing at the Center of Power," *The Washingtonian*, May 1999, pp. 67–73.
4. Colin Powell, "'I Wasn't Left to Myself,'" *Newsweek*, April 27, 1998, p. 32.
5. David Roth, *Sacred Honor: A Biography of Colin Powell* (Grand Rapids, Mich.: Zondervan Publishing House, 1993), p. 32.
6. Colin Powell with Joseph E. Persico, *My American Journey* (New York: Ballantine Books, 1995, revised edition 2003), p. 12.
7. Ibid.
8. Powell, p. 13.

9. Author interview with Gene Norman, November 12, 2003.

10. Ibid.

11. Ibid.

12. Ibid.

13. Colin L. Powell, "From CCNY to The White House," *The City College Alumnus*, Fall 1988, pp. 12–15.

Chapter 3. A College Student's Commitment

1. Colin Powell with Joseph E. Persico, *My American Journey* (New York: Ballantine Books, 1995, revised edition 2003), p. 24.

2. Powell, p. 23.

3. Ibid., p. 25.

4. Author interview with Gene Norman, November 12, 2003.

5. Powell, p. 28.

6. Ibid., p. 25.

7. Author interview with Gene Norman, November 12, 2003.

8. Author interview with Colin Powell, January 2, 2004.

9. Ibid.

10. Colin L. Powell, "From CCNY to The White House," *The City College Alumnus*, Fall 1988, pp. 12–15.

11. Powell, *My American Journey*, p. 27.

12. David Roth, *Sacred Honor: A Biography of Colin Powell* (Grand Rapids, Mich.: Zondervan Publishing House, 1993), p. 41.

13. Ibid., p. 41.

14. Powell, pp. 33–34.

15. Ibid., p. 34.

16. Ibid., p. 35.

CHAPTER NOTES

Chapter 4. "You're in the Army Now"

1. Howard Means, *Colin Powell: Soldier/Statesman, Statesman/Soldier* (New York: Donald I. Fine, Inc., 1992), p. 106.

2. Colin Powell with Joseph E. Persico, *My American Journey* (New York: Ballantine Books, 1995, revised edition 2003), p. 41.

3. Ibid., p. 41.

4. Ibid., p. 51.

5. Colin L. Powell, from the foreword to *Lasting Valor* by Vernon J. Baker with Ken Olsen (New York: Bantam Books, 1999), unpaged.

6. Sandra McElwaine, "Her American Journey," *Ladies Home Journal*, May 1996, pp. 152–153.

Chapter 5. Two Tours of Duty in Vietnam

1. Colin Powell with Joseph E. Persico, *My American Journey* (New York: Ballantine Books, 1995, revised edition 2003), p. 83.

2. Ibid., p. 92.

3. Ibid., p. 96.

4. Ibid., p. 101.

5. Ibid., p. 105.

6. Ibid.

7. Ken Adelman, "What I've Learned: Ground Zero: Colin Powell on War, Peace, and Balancing at the Center of Power," *The Washingtonian*, May 1990, pp. 67–73.

8. Howard Means, *Colin Powell: Soldier/Statesman, Statesman/Soldier* (New York: Donald I. Fine, Inc., 1992), p. 157.

9. Ibid., pp. 143–144.

Chapter 6. The Yo-Yo Years

1. Colin Powell with Joseph E. Persico, *My American Journey* (New York: Ballantine Books, 1995, revised edition 2003), p. 147.

2. "White House Fellows: About the Program: Purpose," *The White House website*, n.d. <http://www.whitehouse.gov/fellows/about/history.html> (August 24, 2003).

3. "The Mission and Structure of the Office of Management and Budget," *Office of Management and Budget website*, n.d. <http://whitehouse.gov/omb/organization/text/mission.html> (September 15, 2003).

4. Powell, p. 172.

5. Howard Means, *Colin Powell: Soldier/Statesman, Statesman/Soldier* (New York: Donald I. Fine, Inc., 1992), p. 181.

6. Author interview with Colin Powell, January 2, 2004.

7. Means, p. 181.

8. David Roth, *Sacred Honor: A Biography of Colin Powell* (Grand Rapids, Mich.: Zondervan Publishing House, 1993), p. 103.

9. Ibid., p. 104.

10. Powell, p. 226.

11. Sara Fritz, "Gen. Powell Faces Toughest Test in Gulf Deployment," *Los Angeles Times*, August 21, 1990, p. A1.

12. Author interview with Frank Carlucci, December 11, 2003.

Chapter 7. **Back in Washington**

1. Caspar W. Weinberger with Gretchen Roberts, *In the Arena: A Memoir of the 20th Century* (Washington, D.C.: Regnery Publishing, Inc., 2001), p. 294.

2. Colin Powell with Joseph E. Persico, *My American Journey* (New York: Ballantine Books, 1995, revised edition 2003), p. 294.

3. "The Economy Act," *U.S. Department of Labor website*, n.d. <http://www.dol.gov/oasam/regs/statutes/1535.htm> (February 22, 2004).

4. Bernard Weintraub, "Reagan Won't Ask Ex-Aides for Details," *The New York Times*, December 9, 1986, p. A14.

5. Powell, p. 318.

6. Author interview with Frank Carlucci, December 11, 2003.

7. Andrew Rosenthal, "A General Who Is Right for His Time," *The New York Times*, August 10, 1989, p. B6.

8. Melissa Healy and James Gerstenzang, "Gen. Powell—Quest for Compromise," *Los Angeles Times*, June 27, 1988, part 1, p. 6.

9. Howard Means, *Colin Powell: Soldier/Statesman, Statesman/Soldier* (New York: Donald I. Fine, Inc., 1992), p. 239.

10. David Roth, *Sacred Honor: A Biography of Colin Powell* (Grand Rapids, Mich.: Zondervan Publishing House, 1993), p. 128.

11. Steven V. Roberts, "General Powell Getting Army's Top Command," *The New York Times*, December 2, 1988, p. B6.

Chapter 8. Chairman of the Joint Chiefs of Staff

1. Colin Powell with Joseph E. Persico, *My American Journey* (New York: Ballantine Books, 1995, revised edition 2003), p. 395.

2. Ibid.

3. Melissa Healy, "Choice of Powell to Head Joint Chiefs Praised," *Los Angeles Times*, August 11, 1989, part 1, p. 4.

4. Ibid.

5. Melissa Healy, "Powell Honors Blacks Who Served," *Los Angeles Times*, August 18, 1989, part 1, p. 4.

6. David Roth, *Sacred Honor: A Biography of Colin Powell* (Grand Rapids, Mich.: Zondervan Publishing House, 1993), p. 162.

7. Michael R. Gordon, "Vital for the Invasion: Politically Attuned General," *The New York Times*, December 25, 1989, p. 9.

8. Bruce W. Nelan, "Ready for Action," *Time*, November 12, 1990, pp. 26–31.

9. Ibid.

10. Powell, p. 575.

Chapter 9. Private Citizen

1. Colin Powell with Joseph E. Persico, *My American Journey* (New York: Ballantine Books, 1995, revised edition 2003), p. 577.

2. Ibid., p. 586.

3. Ibid., p. 287.

4. Elizabeth Kolbert, "With the Country Seeking a Leader, Gen. Powell Explains Who He Is," *The New York Times*, September 17, 1995, p. 20.

5. "Excerpts from Powell's News Conference on Political Plans," *The New York Times*, November 9, 1995, p. B13.

6. Ibid.

7. "Fears for Safety Played No Role in Decision, Mrs. Powell Says," *The New York Times*, November 9, 1995, p. B13.

8. Transcript of speech, "GOP Must Be the 'Party of Inclusion,'" *The Washington Post*, August 13, 1996, p. A15.

9. Elizabeth Shogren, "Powell Urges Mentors for At-Risk Youth," *Los Angeles Times*, April 29, 1997, p. A9.

10. James Bennet, "Look Who's Back in the Ring With Everything but His Hat," *The New York Times*, April 15, 1997, p. A1.

11. Steven Gray, "Gen. Powell Urges City's Schools to Put Children First," *The Washington Post*, August 19, 1998, p. B8.

Chapter 10. Another Return to Public Service

1. Paul Duggan, "Powell Visits Texas 'Friend,' Faces the Usual Questions," *The Washington Post*, May 26, 2000, p. A4.

2. Alison Mitchell, "Bush Rebuffs Warning From an Abortion Foe," *The New York Times*, May 26, 2000, p. A16.

3. *Vital Speeches of the Day*, August 15, 2000, pp. 651–653.

4. "Excerpts From General Powell's Address to Republicans," *The New York Times*, August 1, 2000, p. A18.

5. Mike Allen, "With Eye on Transition, Bush Confers With Powell," *The Washington Post*, December 1, 2000, p. A26.

6. Robin Wright and Edwin Chen, "Powell Promises Active U.S. Role on Global Issues," *Los Angeles Times*, December 17, 2000, p. A1.

7. "Confirmation Hearing by Colin L. Powell," *U.S. Department of State website*, January 17, 2001, <www.state.gov/secretary/rm/2001/443pf.htm> (April 21, 2003).

8. Author interview with Colin Powell, January 2, 2004.

9. "Excerpts of Powell Interview," *The Washington Post*, July 14, 2001, p. A16.

10. "Remarks to the Security Council of the United Nations," *U.S. Department of State website*, September 11, 2002, <http://www.state.gov/secretary/rm/2002/13407.htm> (February 23, 2004).

11. Michael Hirsh, "Powell's Battle," *Newsweek*, September 16, 2002, pp. 29–31.

12. "Remarks at the World Economic Forum," *U.S. Department of State website*, January 26, 2003, <http://www.state.gov/secretary/rm/2003/6869.htm> (February 23, 2004).

13. Ibid.

14. *Time*, January 10, 2005, © 2005 Time Inc., <http://www.time.com/time/verbatim/20050110/7.html (February 10, 2005).

15. "Online NewsHour: Jim Lehrer Interviews Colin Powell, January 13, 2005, <http://www.pbs.org/newshour/bb/fedagencies/jan-june05/powell_1-13.html> (February 10, 2005).

Further Reading

Brown, Warren, and Heather Lehr Wagner.
   Colin Powell: Soldier and Statesman. Philadelphia, Pa.:
   Chelsea House, 2005.

Finlayson, Reggie. *Colin Powell*. Minneapolis, Minn.:
   Lerner, 2004.

Harari, Oren. *The Leadership Secrets of Colin Powell*.
   New York: McGraw-Hill, 2002.

Horn, Geoffrey M. *Colin Powell*. Milwaukee, Wisc.:
   World Almanac Library, 2004.

Wukowits, John F. *Colin Powell*. San Diego, Calif.:
   Lucent Books, Inc., 2000.

Internet Addresses

Academy of Achievement: Colin L. Powell

Profile, biography, interview, and photographs.
  <http://www.achievement.org/autodoc/page/
  pow0bio-1>

America's Promise: A Crusade for Youth

General Powell's Message to America and many links.
  <http://www.americaspromise.org/about/message_
  america.cfm>

U.S. Department of State

Biographical information, current news, quotes, photos,
  and U.S. Department of State links.
  <http://www.state.gov/r/pa/ei/biog/1349.htm>

Index

Page numbers for photographs are in **boldface** type.